shakespeare's
the merchant of venice

shakespeare's
the merchant of venice

harold bloom

riverhead books
new york

THE BERKLEY PUBLISHING GROUP
Published by the Penguin Group
Penguin Group (USA) Inc.
375 Hudson Street, New York, New York 10014, USA
Penguin Group (Canada), 10 Alcorn Avenue, Toronto, Ontario, Canada M4V 3B2
(a division of Pearson Penguin Canada Inc.)
Penguin Books Ltd., 80 Strand, London WC2R 0RL, England
Penguin Group Ireland, 25 St. Stephen's Green, Dublin 2, Ireland (a division of Penguin Books, Ltd.)
Penguin Group (Australia), 250 Camberwell Road, Camberwell, Victoria 3124, Australia
(a division of Pearson Australia Group Pty., Ltd.)
Penguin Books India Pvt. Ltd., 11 Community Centre, Panchsheel Park, New Delhi—110 017, India
Penguin Group (NZ), Cnr. Airborne and Rosedale Roads, Albany, Auckland 1310, New Zealand
(a division of Pearson New Zealand, Ltd.)
Penguin Books (South Africa) (Pty.) Ltd., 24 Sturdee Avenue, Rosebank, Johannesburg 2196,
South Africa

Penguin Books Ltd., Registered Offices: 80 Strand, London, WC2R 0RL, England

Shakespeare's The Merchant of Venice

PRINTING HISTORY
Riverhead trade paperback edition: July 2005
Riverhead trade paperback ISBN: 1-59448-091-5

This book has been catalogued with the Library of Congress.

PRINTED IN THE UNITED STATES OF AMERICA

10   9   8   7   6   5   4   3   2   1

contents

The text of *The Merchant of Venice*, including the synopsis, is that of the old Cambridge Edition (1893), as edited by William Aldis Wright. I am grateful to Brett Foster for indispensable advice upon the editorial revisions I have made in the text.

—Harold Bloom

harold bloom on
the merchant of venice

One would have to be blind, deaf, and dumb not to recognize that Shakespeare's grand, equivocal comedy *The Merchant of Venice* is nevertheless a profoundly anti-Semitic work. Yet every time I have taught the play, many of my most sensitive and intelligent students become very unhappy when I begin with that observation. Nor do they accept my statements that Shylock is a comic villain and that Portia would cease to be sympathetic if Shylock were allowed to be a figure of overwhelming pathos. That Shakespeare himself was personally anti-Semitic we reasonably can doubt, but Shylock is one of those Shakespearean figures who seem to break clean away from their plays' confines. There is an extraordinary energy in Shylock's prose and poetry, a force both cognitive and passional, which palpably is in excess of the play's comic requirements. More even than Marlowe's Barabas, Jew of Malta, Shylock is a villain both farcical and scary, though time has worn away both qualities. Shakespeare's England did not exactly have a Jewish "problem" or "question" in our later modern terms; only about a hundred or two hundred Jews, presumably most of them converts to Christianity, lived in London. The Jews had been more or less expelled from England in 1290, three centuries before, and were not to be more or less readmitted until Cromwell made his revolution. The unfortunate Dr. Lopez, Queen Elizabeth's physician, was hanged, drawn, and quartered (possibly with Shakespeare among the mob looking on), having been more or less framed by the Earl of Essex and so perhaps falsely accused of a plot to poison the Queen. A Portuguese *converso,* whom Shakespeare may have known, poor Lopez lives on as a shadowy provocation to the highly successful revival of Marlowe's *The Jew of Malta* in 1593–94, and presumably to Shakespeare's eventual overcoming of Marlowe in *The Merchant of Venice,* perhaps in 1596–97.

Shakespeare's comedy is Portia's play, and not Shylock's, though some audiences now find it difficult to reach that conclusion. Antonio, the title's merchant, is the good Christian of the play, who manifests his piety by cursing and spitting at Shylock. For many among us now, that is at least an irony, but clearly it was no irony for Shakespeare's audiences. I have never seen *The Merchant of Venice* staged with Shylock as comic villain, but that is certainly how the play should be performed. Shylock would be very bad news indeed if he were not funny; since he doesn't provoke *us* to laughter, we play him for pathos, as he has been played since the early nineteenth century, except in Germany and Austria under the Nazis, and in Japan. I am afraid that we tend to make *The Merchant of Venice* incoherent by portraying Shylock as being largely sympathetic. Yet I myself am puzzled as to what it would cost (and not only ethically) to recover the play's coherence. Probably it would cost us Shakespeare's actual Shylock, who cannot have been quite what Shakespeare intended, if indeed we can recover such an intention. If I were a director, I would instruct my Shylock to act like a hallucinatory bogeyman, a walking nightmare flamboyant with a big false nose and a bright red wig, that is to say, to *look* like Marlowe's Barabas. We can imagine the surrealistic effect of such a figure when he begins to speak with the nervous intensity, the realistic energy of Shylock, who is so much of a personality as to at least rival his handful of lively precursors in Shakespeare: Faulconbridge the Bastard in *King John,* Mercutio and the Nurse in *Romeo and Juliet,* and Bottom the Weaver in *A Midsummer Night's Dream.* But these characters all fit their roles, even if we can conceive of them as personalities outside of their plays. Shylock simply does not fit his role; he is the wrong Jew in the right play.

I suggest that to understand the gap between the human that Shakespeare invents and the role that as playmaker he condemns Shylock to act, we regard the Jew of Venice as a reaction formation or ironic swerve away from Marlowe's Jew of Malta. All that Shylock and Barabas have in common is that both are supposed to be not Jews, but *the* Jew. Shakespeare's grim Puritan and Marlowe's ferocious Machiavel are so antithetical to each other that I have always wanted a mischievous director slyly to transfer crucial declarations between them. How disconcertingly splendid it would be to have Shylock suddenly burst out with Barabas's most outrageous parody of Jewish wickedness:

> As for myself, I walk abroad a–nights,
> And kill sick people groaning under walls;
> Sometimes I go about and poison wells.

That is the superb cartoon that Shakespeare parodied again in Aaron the Moor of *Titus Andronicus,* and such savage zest cannot be repeated by Shylock, who is not a phantasmagoria, even when he behaves like one. The counterstroke would be to have Barabas cry out, "If you prick us, do we not bleed? If you tickle us, do we not laugh?" which may or may not be poignant when delivered by Shylock but certainly would destroy Barabas's antic irreality.

Shakespeare, finished at last with Marlowe, contrasts against the cartoon Barabas Shylock's realistic mimesis, which is so over-whelming that it cannot be accommodated as a stage Jew. Yet Shakespeare wants it both ways, at once to push Marlowe aside, and also to so out-Marlowe Marlowe as to make our flesh creep. The stunning persuasiveness of Shylock's personality heightens our apprehension of watching a stage Jew slice off and weigh a pound of the good Antonio's flesh—"to bait fish withal." If the audience has a surrogate in this drama, it would appear to be Gratiano, whose anti-Semitic vulgarity reminds me of Julius Streicher, Hitler's favorite newspaper editor. The last two cen-turies of stage tradition have made Shylock a hero-villain, but the text cannot sustain such an interpretation. Since Shylock is a murderous villain, then Gratiano, though a touch crude, must be taken as a good fellow, cheerful and robust in his anti-Semitism, a kind of Pat Buchanan of Renaissance Venice.

Shakespearean skeptical irony, so pervasive elsewhere in *The Merchant of Venice,* perhaps goes into relative suspension when-ever Shylock speaks. Shylock's prose is Shakespeare's best before Falstaff's; Shylock's verse hews to the vernacular more than any in Shakespeare before Hamlet's. The bitter eloquence of Shylock so impresses us that it is always a surprise to be told how small a part of the play is spoken by him: only 360 lines and sentences. His utterances manifest a spirit so potent, malign, and negative as to be unforgettable. Yet it is spirit, albeit the spirit of resentment and revenge. I doubt that Shakespeare knew enough about the post-biblical history of the Jews to have meditated upon it, and therefore Shylock cannot be said to embody Jewish history, ex-cept for the unhappy truth that Shakespeare's power has con-verted much of later Jewish history into Shylock. It would have been better for the Jews, if not for most of *The Merchant of Venice*'s audiences, had Shylock been a character less conspicu-ously alive. What spurred Shakespeare to that liveliness, as I've already intimated, was the contest with Marlowe's Barabas. But what is it that provoked Shakespeare's inventiveness?

Perhaps it is the wicked small boy in me that so delights in Barabas; Marlowe certainly delighted in his Jew, who is as close to aspects of Marlowe's temperament as Shylock is distant from Shakespeare's, if Falstaff is as much the Shakespearean norm as I take him to be. Barabas, of course, is no more Jewish than the play's Christians are Christian or its Muslims Muslim. Shakespeare disturbs me because his influence has been so universal that Shylock seems Jewish to many audiences, though the figure they see has been converted into one of heroic pathos. When we think of the Jew in post-biblical literature, George Eliot's Daniel Deronda, Dickens's Fagin, and Joyce's half-Jewish Poldy, among others, come to mind only *after* we brood upon Shylock. No one, except the incessantly anti-Semitic T. S. Eliot, has tended to think of Barabas as a truly Jewish character. Barabas is a kind of wicked bottle imp or Jew-in-the-box; he is always jumping out at us, the audience. We can't help enjoying him, since his outrageousness is so cartoon-like. But I will return to Barabas later, in the context of Shakespeare's revision of Marlowe for his own rather different purposes.

We finally have a lucid and sound study of *The Merchant of Venice* in *Shakespeare and the Jews,* by James Shapiro (1996), whose "Conclusion" is worthy of much meditation:

I have tried to show that much of the play's vitality can be attributed to the ways in which it scrapes against a bedrock of beliefs about the racial, national, sexual, and religious difference of others. I can think of no other literary work that does so as unrelentingly and as honestly. To avert our gaze from what the play reveals about the relationship between cultural myths and peoples' identities will not make irrational and exclusionary attitudes disappear. Indeed, these darker impulses remain so elusive, so hard to identify in the normal course of things, that only in instances like productions of this play do we get to glimpse these cultural faultlines. This is why censoring the play is *always* more dangerous than staging it.

"Censoring," of course, is usually not the issue, except in Nazi Germany and in Israel, as Shapiro shows. What baffles us is how to stage a romantic comedy that rather blithely includes a forced Jewish conversion to Christianity, on penalty of death. When Shylock brokenly intones, "I am content," few of our audiences are going to be content, unless you can conjure up a cheerfully anti-Semitic audience somewhere. *King Lear* is a pagan play for a Christian audience, some scholars like to say. *The Merchant of Venice* is a Christian play for a Christian audience, according to Northrop Frye. I don't think that Shakespeare wrote Christian plays, or un-Christian ones either, and as I have written earlier, my sense of the endlessly perspectivizing Shakespeare would exclude the possibility that he was personally either anti-Semitic or philo-Semitic, which is also Shapiro's conclusion. It is difficult for me not to assent to Graham Bradshaw's fine contention that Shakespeare's "creative interiorization of Shylock" makes unlikely any views that see the Jewish merchant as being entirely a comic villain or only a figure of tragic pathos. What drives me back to a state of critical unhappiness is Shakespeare's disconcerting addition to the pound-of-flesh story: the forced conversion. It is Shakespeare's own invention, and I never find it dramatically persuasive that Shylock should consent to it. Portia may have broken Shylock, but she has not pulverized him, and it is no longer Shylock who stumbles off stage, soon to be a new Christian, or a false Christian, or whatever. Why did Shakespeare allow Antonio this final turn of the torturer's screw?

Had Shylock grown too large for the play, in Shakespeare's

wary intuition, so that he needed to be removed, as Mercutio and Lear's Fool and Lady Macbeth are exiled? This seems dubious to me, if only because Shakespeare has waited too long in the play to exile Shylock. "He should have converted hereafter," we are likely to mutter, knowing that there would have been no such time. It is not like Shakespeare to blunder into a theatrical coup that makes even a comic villain behave with dramatic inconsistency. Malvolio, in a madman's cell, maintains his integrity, but Shylock, hemmed in by enemies, is not permitted to do so. Once I believed this to be a relatively rare Shakespearean error; now I suspect otherwise. Shakespeare needs the conversion, not so much to reduce Shylock as to take the audience off to Belmont without a Jewish shadow hovering in the ecstatic if gently ironic final act.

There is nothing lyrical about Shylock, and no place for him in Belmont. But what was Shakespeare to do with Shylock? Hanging, drawing, and quartering, or similar open-air entertainment, would be a poor prelude to Belmont. We cannot know precisely what Shakespeare the man thought of actual Jewish individual "conversions," but he was unlikely to be less skeptical of them than were almost all his contemporaries. It had been more than a century since the Spanish Expulsion of the Jews, a debacle partly caused by Christian awareness of massive Jewish recalcitrance and tendency to dissimulate when compelled to convert. Shapiro views Shylock's conversion as an answer to English Protestant anxieties, which contained the expectation of a mass conversion of the Jews, which would help confirm the Reformation's rightness. The relevance of such a Christian fantasy to The Merchant of Venice seems to me quite tenuous, since the Belmont joys of Act V are deliciously secular, nor is Shylock's forced conversion in any way a possible harbinger of a messianic age. We feel that Shakespeare intended an idiosyncratic end for Shylock, more as punishment than as redemption, and there may be the clue. Forced conversions on an individual basis were very rare phenomena, as Shapiro's researches confirm. Shakespeare, with Marlowe's Barabas in mind, does not give Shylock the option of declaring, "I will be no convertite," as Barabas does. His destroying Shylock's consistency as a character helps further to distinguish him from the unyielding Barabas, and helps also to augment the nihilistic element that is subtly present in the play. No one in *The Merchant of Venice* is what he or she seems to be—not Portia, Antonio, Bassanio, or Jessica—and can Shakespeare allow only Shylock to maintain a consistent stance? Who in this comedy can have his or her bond? A Sixth Act would dissolve Belmont into moonlight wiped away like mud. Shylock accepts conversion because the Venice of this play, like the Vienna of *Measure for Measure,* is too equivocal for any consistency to prevail. It is *The Merchant of Venice*'s finest irony that the alien Shylock is never more Venetian than when he sells himself out. What is his motive? Do we misread his "I am content" when we fail to hear a terrible irony in it? Has Shylock perhaps learned so much from Christian justice that he is prepared to move his struggle to a more inward mode of resistance?

We can only surmise, in this comedy set in a city of psychic dark corners. Despite the Belmont fifth act, *The Merchant of Venice* may be Shakespeare's first "dark comedy" or "problem play," forerunner of *All's Well That Ends Well, Troilus and Cressida,* and *Measure for Measure,* with their equivocal groupings of Helena, Bertram, and Parolles; Pandarus, Thersites, and Ulysses; Duke Vincentio, Isabella, and Lucio. Antonio, as so many critics observe, is Shylock's mirror image, bonded with him in mutual hatred, and no more cheerful than Shylock is. Portia, the play's center, is far more complex and shadowed than ever I have seen her played as being. Herself a sophisticated ironist, she settles happily for the glittering gold digger Bassanio, contemptuously sentences poor Morocco and Aragon to celibate existences, and is delighted with her Belmont and her Venice alike. More even than the vicious Gratiano, she incarnates the "anything goes" spirit of Venice, and her quality of mercy cheerfully tricks Shylock out of his life's savings in order to enrich her friends. Our directors go on instructing our actresses to play Portia as if she was Rosalind, which is a malfeasance. Bradshaw finds a touch of Henry James worldliness in Portia, but we would render her better by invoking Noël Coward or Cole Porter. I am not proposing that someone give us *The Merchant of Venice* as the first anti-Semitic musical comedy, but I do suggest that Portia, who knows better, consistently is delighted to fail all her own finely wrought self-awareness. Her moral fiber is Jamesian, but her sense of the high life wryly allows her to settle for Bassanio and tricksterism. She is rather wonderful bad news, a slummer by joyous choice. Yes, she has the wit to flatten Shylock, Jew and alien, but her city, Venice, is completely on her side, and the obsessed Shylock is entirely on his own. He gets about what he deserves, except for that gratuitous forced conversion, which Portia happily endorses, but which is Antonio's idea, and not hers. She is at worst a happy hypocrite, far too intelligent not to see that she is not exactly dispensing Christian mercy, except by Venetian standards. Antonio is quite another matter; he is ironically the play's best Christian, a champion spitter-at and kicker-of Jews. If one is Jewish, one is hardly his intended audience, let alone his contemplated critic, even if one does not wish a pound of his Pauline heart or of his Venetian privates.

In this endlessly ironic play, the melancholy Antonio finishes with little except regained riches and his triumphant anti-Semitism to cheer him. Indeed, his sexual fate is precisely that of the Princes of Morocco and Aragon, perpetual celibacy, since Bassanio will be otherwise engaged in servicing Portia. Still, Antonio is at Belmont, surrounded by three pairs of lovers, while his enemy Shylock is in Venice, doubtless receiving instruction in

Catholicism. Christian comedy triumphs, Jewish villainy is thwarted, and everything is for the best, if only Shylock's voice and presence would stop reverberating, which they never have and never will, four centuries after Shakespeare composed, and in the centuries to come. Had Hitler won the Second World War and gone on to add ten million more Jews to his achievement of six million Jewish corpses, then Shylock would have ceased to reverberate, but his unhappy persistence will extend as long as the history of the Jews, in which he has played an inglorious part, hardly one that Shakespeare ever could have contemplated. Early modern anti-Semitism was not pretty; the good Antonio and the loud Gratiano will stand as poor Shylock's godfathers at the baptismal font, though Gratiano would rather hang him, and Antonio is not at all likely to stop kicking and spitting, Venetian Christianity being what it was and is. Shakespeare, we can assume, was Shakespeare's most gifted critic, and he would have been aware that Shylock, comic or not, was a grander achievement than Antonio could be. Still, Antonio is a dark matter, and requires some contemplation if his adversary Shylock is to be properly perspectivized.

Antonio lives for Bassanio and indeed is willing to die for him, and mortgages his pound of flesh to Shylock solely so that Bassanio can deck his good looks out in order to wive it wealthily in Belmont. Bassanio is not a bad fellow, but no one would want to try the project of distinguishing between Bassanio and Lorenzo, two Venetian playboys in search of heiresses. It is true that all Shakespeare's heroines are condemned to marry down, but if you compare Portia's Bassanio to Rosalind's Orlando, obviously you will prefer the amiable young wrestler of *As You Like It* to the sincere fortune hunter of *The Merchant of Venice*. Notoriously, Portia's play, and Portia herself, and her friends, are all about money. Belmont is delightful, and obviously very expensive, and Portia, while wiser than Jessica, Nerissa, Gratiano,

Lorenzo, and Bassanio, requires no loftier company than these well-dressed sophisticates. I never know what critics think they are talking about when they find transcendent virtues in Portia's Belmont. John Middleton Murry, admirable interpreter of Keats and of Blake, wrote a lesser study, *Shakespeare* (1936), in which he affirmed that "*The Merchant of Venice* is not a problem play; it is a fairy story." I murmur, when I read this, that I don't expect fairy stories to be anti-Semitic, though of course there are a few. More to the point is that Portia and her friends, in Act V, are not exactly partying in a pumpkin, or in a gingerbread house, but in a great hall, being serenaded by musicians, with a trumpet sounding at each fresh arrival. Once the pretty matter of the rings has been gotten through, thus reassuring Portia that she has priority over Antonio in Bassanio's affections, the only crucial question is whether to stay up partying until dawn or go to bed and get on with it. Everyone is a lot fresher than they were going to be four centuries later in *La Dolce Vita*, but basically they are the same set.

Antonio, though he is there in Belmont, will go to bed alone, presumably comforted by his altruism, his piety, and his triumph over Shylock. Bassanio, we have to assume, is bisexual, but Antonio clearly is not, and his homoeroticism is perhaps less relevant than his sadomasochism, the doom-eagerness that could allow him to make so mad a contract with Shylock. If the comedy has a hero, to rival Portia as heroine, it has to be Antonio, and not the lightweight Bassanio, charming and harmless fellow. But I've never met anyone who much likes Antonio, quite aside from his compulsive tendency to kick and spit at passing Jews. We want for Shylock's antagonist a somewhat more engaging merchant of Venice, who has something other than his Christianity to recommend him. Leslie Fielder once wrote that Antonio was a "projection of the author's private distress," which counts as interesting guesswork but no more. Various critics have found Antonio to be a gull, a Christ figure, a self-victimizer, and much else, and clearly he is rather an ambiguous character. But all that makes him vivid and memorable is the quality of the mutual hatred he shares with Shylock. As a hater, he is outclassed by Shylock, but then he achieves a certain stature by coming up with the idea of the forced conversion. That, and the notorious pound of flesh near his heart, are what matter about him, and one has to question whether Shakespeare, for whatever reason, failed to do enough with the interior Antonio.

However problematic, *The Merchant of Venice* essentially is a romantic comedy, and pathos is alien to it, as alien as Shylock the Jew. I myself find little pathos in Shylock, and am not moved by his "Hath not a Jew" litany, since what he is saying there is now of possible interest only to wavering skinheads and similar sociopaths. Perhaps it was a revelation for Shakespeare's audience, but it had better not be such for any audience now. Shylock matters where he is most formidable, as when he faces the Duke of Venice, and insists that he will have his bond. Let us dismiss the notion, Northrop Frye's weakest, that Shylock speaks for the Old Testament and Portia for the merciful New Covenant. Frye was a great critic but not when he mixed criticism with being a Low Church clergyman, just as T. S. Eliot's criticism did not benefit from his High Church proclivities. Deuteronomy forbids what Shylock seeks to do, and may God (and democracy) save me from Portia's mercy! Portia is dangerously theatrical, and not just when she is cross-dressing. She shares this trait with her lover, Bassanio, and with her rival, Antonio. Shylock oddly is not at all theatrical, dramatically superb as he is until his unlikely conversion. His menace and his now-lost comic force depend upon the contrast between his monomaniacal sincerity and the engaging frivolity of Portia's Venetian smart set. To reduce him to contemporary theatrical terms, Shylock would be an Arthur Miller protagonist displaced into a Cole Porter musical, Willy Loman wandering about in *Kiss Me Kate*.

Shakespeare specialized in such displaced spirits, and in this one regard Shylock has affinities with a strikingly varied company that includes Malvolio, Caliban, Lear's Fool, Barnardine, and even an aspect of Falstaff. Malvolio, in a play by Ben Jonson, almost would be Jonson, but in *Twelfth Night,* his displacement makes him the comic butt. I assume that Shylock began in *The Merchant of Venice* as a similar comic figure, in Shakespeare's design, but Shylock kindled Shakespeare's imagination and became enlarged beyond comedy, though into menace rather than pathos. The stimulus for Shylock's metamorphosis had to be Marlowe's Barabas, who had been haunting Shakespeare since his beginnings as a dramatist.

Shylock is an anti–Barabas, turned inward, as much a deep psyche as Barabas is a cartoon. Shakespeare's imitations of Barabas, Aaron the Moor and Richard III, do homage to Marlowe, but Shylock exposes Barabas as a mere caricature, however brilliant and ferocious. "I'll show you the Jew," Shakespeare says in reply to Marlowe, and so, alas, he has, to the everlasting harm of the actual Jewish people. This is hardly to say that Shylock is a valid representation of a Jew, let alone the Jew, but it does acknowledge the scandalous authority of Shakespeare in world culture, an authority that just this once is more of a sorrow than it is a benefit. *The Jew of Malta* is still a lively romp, much admired by T. S. Eliot, though I suspect for the wrong reasons, since Eliot doubtless treasured it as an anti–Semitic farce, which it is not. Its Christians and Muslims come off far worse than Barabas, since they would be just as wicked if they could but lack Barabas's genius for evil. Marlowe's Jew is simply Christopher Marlowe gone all out into lunatic zest and diabolic energy, overturning all values and sending up everything and everyone. A great holiday from reality, *The Jew of Malta* exalts active evil over passive good, and can be called the *Ubu Roi* of its time, the first Pataphysical drama. In his stage directions, Jarry remarked: "The action takes place nowhere—that is to say, in

Poland," perhaps the first of modern Polish jokes. In the same spirit, Marlowe's action (such as it is) takes place in Malta—that is to say, nowhere. Marlowe had no literary or historical sources for *The Jew of Malta,* which could take place almost anywhere in the Mediterranean, in any one of several centuries, but only after Machiavel, who wonderfully steps forward in the play's prologue, to urge our acclaim of Barabas. Like his master, Machiavel, Marlowe's Jew is obsessed with "policy"—that is, with principles that undo Christ. The demoniac Barabas, madly exulting in his wickedness, has nothing in common with the bitter Shylock, whose revenge focuses so narrowly upon Antonio.

Shakespeare works assiduously to exclude any Marlovian element from Shylock, but that inevitably entails a journey to the Shylockian interior. Barabas is free of all inwardness; Shylock, in recoil, is so concentrated in his inward power that he reduces Portia and her friends, and even Antonio, to what can look like exercises in irony. The phenomenon of a "real" person entrapped in a play, surrounded by speaking shadows, is strongest in *Hamlet,* evidently by design. Yet the aesthetic experiment of the Pirandello-like mode, perfected in *Hamlet,* is first ventured in *The Merchant of Venice,* where the ontological weight of Shylock, from his first appearance through his last, places him as a representation of reality far distaining every other character in the play. Shylock, equivocal as he must be, is our best clue for tracing the process by which Shakespeare outdid Marlowe, and in doing so invented or reinvented the human.

Barabas is exuberant, but he is a monster, not a man. Shakespeare's obsessed Shylock is compulsive enough in his hatred of Antonio so that he would have performed monstrously, but for Portia; yet Shylock is no monster but an overwhelming persuasion of a possible human being. Shylock matters most not just in the historical world of anti-Semitism, but also in the inner world of Shakespeare's development, because no previous figure in the plays has anything like Shylock's strength, complexity, and vital potential. Shylock's pathos can be termed his *potentia,* his possible largeness on the scale of being. That so resourceful a spirit should have reduced itself to a lust for weighing out a pound of Antonio's flesh upon a literal scale is the most terrible of Shakespeare's ironies in this comedy of ironies.

There remains Shylock's largest puzzle, at least for me: Is he the first radical Shakespearean instance of Hobgoblin run off with the garland of Apollo? Is Shylock of the literary race of Falstaff and of Dickens's Pickwick, the tribe in which Don Quixote, Sancho Panza, and Hamlet share with Falstaff the highest eminence? Can Shakespeare be said to have lost control of Shylock? Nothing after all sounds odder than to call Shylock a comic villain, like the zestful Barabas, even though *The Merchant of Venice,* however shaded, is still a comedy, and the Jewish moneylender is certainly its villain. In refusing to create another Aaron the Moor or Richard III, both imitations of Barabas, Shakespeare molded Shylock into someone rich and strange, in several senses. Barabas's principal affect is self-delight, a joy provoked by his own triumphant and antic villainy. Aaron and Richard Crookback also enjoy themselves to the highest degree, but Shylock takes little pleasure in himself or anything else, despite his pride in his self-identity. Critics frequently mark the sadness that is common to Antonio and to Shylock, an involuntary link between good haters of each other. Though the sadness be mutual, the causes are very different; Antonio, whatever his relations with Bassanio may have been, must lose him to Portia, while Shylock evidently has long mourned his wife Leah, mother of the insufferable Jessica, the Venetian Jewish princess who gets what she deserves in her playboy, Lorenzo. Shakespeare does not clarify Shylock's relationship to his thieving daughter, but he is certainly better off without her, and is accurate enough in grieving equally for his ducats and their appropriator.

We adore Barabas, Aaron, and even Richard III because their asides make us their accomplices. Shakespeare, to prevent this, never allows us to be alone with Shylock. Barabas dissembles, and consciously always gives a performance; Shylock is massively, frighteningly sincere and singleminded. He never acts a part: he *is* Shylock. Though this endows him with immense expressive force, it also makes him dreadfully vulnerable, and inevitably metamorphoses him into the play's scapegoat. He is capable of shattering irony, particularly in his speeches to the Duke, but the comedy's largest irony makes him its victim. Portia is the privileged ironist of *The Merchant of Venice*, but she becomes a brutal ironist at Shylock's expense, though not as brutal as the good Antonio, who offers Shylock a choice between a pauper's execution and a Christian's survival as a retired moneylender, since a converted Shylock by definition cannot engage in a purely Jewish business.

Shakespeare, rather more subtly than Marlowe, shows that though the Christians (except for Gratiano) are more refined than Shylock, they are hardly more merciful. Portia is a great charmer, but then Bassanio, Lorenzo, Nerissa, and Jessica are also charming, if rather emptier than Portia. Shylock is a candidate for the least charming character in all of Shakespeare, yet he fascinates us, and for reasons that transcend his transparent villainy. His language, an extraordinary instrument, had to impress Shakespeare as a dramatic breakthrough for the poet-playwright. We do not encounter Shylock until Act I, Scene iii, after we already know Antonio, Bassanio, and Portia, and we first hear Shylock speaking a virtuoso prose culminating in his refusal of Bassanio's civil invitation to dinner:

Yes, to smell pork, to eat of the habitation which your prophet the Nazarite conjured the devil into: I will buy with you, sell with you, talk with you, walk with you, and

so following: but I will not eat with you, drink with you,
nor pray with you.

[I.iii.29–33]

The reference to the Gospel of Mark, like the one to Luke
when Shylock sees Antonio coming, provides the odd detail that
Shakespeare's Jew has read the enemy Scripture. And indeed
Shylock is a formidable polemicist against Christianity, particularly against what passes for Christian ethics in Venice. Less in-
flammatory than Marlowe's Jew, Shylock is at least as stubbornly
loyal to his people as Barabas is, making his consent to the final,
forced conversion almost absurdly inconsistent. His first speech
in verse, a rare aside, invokes an archaic enmity, reaching back far
beyond Antonio and Shylock:

If I can catch him once upon the hip,
I will feed fat the ancient grudge I bear him.
He hates our sacred nation, and he rails
(Even there where merchants most do congregate)
On me, my bargains, and my well-won thrift,
Which he calls interest: cursed be my tribe
If I forgive him!

[I.iii.41–47]

Shylock asserts his identity as *the* Jew, inheritor of the perse-
cuted pride of fifteen centuries, in lines that burn with a terrify-
ing spiritual rancor, and that are animated by what must be called
a formidable spiritual intelligence. I greatly regret agreeing with
the resentful legions of cultural materialists and cultural poeti-
cians, all of whom have a particular grudge against the criticism
of E.M.W. Tillyard, but no one ever has been more mistaken on
Shylock than Tillyard, who allowed himself to speak of Shylock's
"spiritual stupidity," and of Antonio's "disinterested kindness."

That was in 1965, but it never seems too late in the day for English anti-Semitism to manifest itself. Disinterested kicking and spitting we can set aside; Shylock's spirit is diseased, distorted by hatred, however justified, but Shylock's intelligence, in any sphere, is unquestionable. He would not be so dreadfully dangerous as he is were he not a psychologist of some genius, a precursor of the great critic Iago, and of the superb nihilist Edmund in *King Lear*.

Shylock's companion in hatred is Antonio, whose anti-Semitism, though appropriate to the play's Venice, nevertheless is more viciously intense than anyone else's, even Gratiano's. Homosexual anti-Semitism is now too peculiar a malady for us to understand; from Proust onward the situations of Jews and homosexuals have tended to converge, symbolically and sometimes literally, as in Nazi Germany. Venice and Belmont alike float upon money, and Antonio's attempt to distinguish between his mercantilism and Shylock's usury persuades nobody. The merchant and the Jew perform a murderous dance of masochist and sadist, murderee and murderer, and the question of which is the merchant and which the Jew is resolved only by the unbelievable conversion. Antonio wins and has nothing except money; Shylock loses (and deserves to lose) and has nothing, not even an identity. We cannot interpret his "I am content" because we cannot get out of our ears his two greatest speeches, each directed against Venice—the "gaping pig" rhapsody and the oration on Venetian slavery. Neither speech is necessary for comic completion, and neither is an exercise in pathos. Shakespeare drives his creation to its limit, as if to discover just what kind of character he has limned in Shylock, a night piece that was his best until he revised Hamlet from another wily trickster to a new kind of man.

The transformation of Shylock from a comic villain to a heroic villain (rather than a hero-villain, like Barabas) shows

Shakespeare working without precedents, and for dramatic mo-
tives very difficult to surmise. Shylock always has been a great
role: one thinks of Macklin, Kean, and Irving, though there does
not appear to have been an overwhelming performance in our
own time. I could never come to terms with Olivier's suave
philoSemitic Shylock, who seemed to emanate from Freud's Vienna and not at all from Shakespeare's Venice. The top hat and
black tie had replaced the Jewish gaberdine, and the powerful
speeches of menace were modulated into civilization and its dis-
contents. Though the effect of this was quietly and persuasively
irrealistic, the context for Shylock's passionate nihilism seemed
withdrawn when the shocking lines came forth:

> You'll ask me why I rather choose to have
> A weight of carrion flesh than to receive
> Three thousand ducats: I'll not answer that!
> But say it is my humour,—is it answer'd?
> What if my house be troubled with a rat,
> And I be pleas'd to give ten thousand ducats
> To have it ban'd? what, are you answer'd yet?
> Some men there are love not a gaping pig!
> Some that are mad if they behold a cat!
> And others when the bagpipe sings i'th'nose,
> Cannot contain their urine—for affection
> [ ] of passion sways it to the mood
> Of what it likes or loathes,—now for your answer:
> As there is no firm reason to be rend'red
> Why he cannot abide a gaping pig,
> Why he a harmless necessary cat,
> Why he a woollen bagpipe, but of force
> Must yield to such inevitable shame,
> As to offend, himself being offended:
> So can I give no reason, nor I will not,

More than a lodg'd hate, and a certain loathing
I bear Antonio, that I follow thus
A losing suit against him!—are you answered?

[IV.i.40–62]

The missing word is something like "master," and since Shylock's "affection" primarily means an innate antipathy, while his "passion" means any authentic feeling, he thus portrays himself, quite ironically, as being unable to govern his own will. But Shakespeare's irony goes against Shylock, since Shylock is playing the Christian's game, and cannot win at it: "A lodg'd hate, and a certain loathing" is an excellent definition of anti-Semitism, and Shylock, out of control, has become what he beheld in Antonio, a Jewish terrorist responding to incessant anti-Jewish provocations. But the images of Shylock's speech are more memorable than is his defense of his own vagaries. Antonio's anti-Shylockism and Shylock's anti-Antonioism are parallel instances to the madness of those who lose control when they encounter a gaping pig, become insane at seeing a harmless necessary cat, or involuntarily urinate when the bagpipe sings. What Shylock defiantly celebrates is compulsiveness for its own sake, or traumatic caprice. As a negative psychologist, Shakespeare's Jew prepares us for the abysses of the will in greater Shakespearean villains to come, but Shakespeare has divested Shylock of the grandeur of negative transcendence that will inform Iago, Edmund, and Macbeth. It is the "gaping pig" speech, more than the wounded cry "I will have my bond," that exposes Shylock's emptying-out of his self.

We know next to nothing about the dynamics of Shakespeare's personal relationships, if any, to the great roles he composed. The pattern of the Falstaff-Hal ambivalence seems not unlike the ambivalence sketched in the Sonnets, while the image of Shakespeare's son Hamnet Shakespeare may in some still unknown way contribute to the enigmas of Prince Hamlet. It is

scarcely conceivable that Shylock was any kind of a personal bur-
den to Shakespeare, who essentially belongs to his age, just this
once, in regard to the Jews. Since he is not Marlowe, writing a
bloody farce, Shakespeare is either vicious or ignorant (or both)
when he has Shylock urge Tubal to meet him at the synagogue in
order to work out the details for the judicial murder of Antonio.
Still, both the viciousness and the ignorance were generic, which
does not make them more forgivable. The plot required a Jew,
Marlowe's Jew lingered on the stage, and Shakespeare needed to
fight free of Marlowe. I surmise that Shakespeare's pride at having done just that increased his dramatic investment in Shylock,
and helps account for the most astonishing speech in the play.
When the Duke asks: "How shalt thou hope for mercy rend'ring
none?" Shylock replies with preternatural power, invoking the
ultimate foundation for the Venetian state economy, which is the
ownership of slaves:

> What judgment shall I dread doing no wrong?
> You have among you many a purchas'd slave,
> Which (like your asses, and your dogs and mules)
> You use in abject and in slavish parts,
> Because you bought them—shall I say to you,
> Let them be free, marry them to your heirs?
> Why sweat they under burthens? let their beds
> Be made as soft as yours, and let their palates
> Be season'd with such viandes? you will answer
> "The slaves are ours,"—so do I answer you:
> The pound of flesh (which I demand of him)
> Is dearly bought, 'tis mine and I will have it:
> If you deny me, fie upon your law!
> There is no force in the decrees of Venice:
> I stand for judgment,—answer, shall I have it?

[IV.i.89–103]

It is all too easy to get this speech wrong, as some recent Marxist critics have done. Shylock has no sympathy for the slaves, and he seems quite unaware of the irony his citation of the slaves evokes, since as a Jew he annually celebrates the Passover, with its opening reminder that his ancestors were slaves in Egypt until God liberated them. It is never wise to assume that Shakespeare did not know anything that was available in or near his world; his curiosity was unappeasable, his energy for information boundless. Shylock really does *mean* his ghastly parallel: one pound of Antonio's flesh is enslaved to him, and he will have his bond. What startles and delights us is Shylock's shrewd indictment of Christian hypocrisy, which he makes earlier in the play, but not with this shocking force. The Venetian slaves, like all slaves, are so many pounds of flesh; no more, no less. And in the context of Gingrich-Clinton America, the satire still works: our pious reformers of Welfare are determined to see that the descendants of our slaves do not lie down in beds as soft as theirs, and season their palates with such viands, let alone marry the heirs of the Contract with America. Yet Shylock does not care about his own fiercest point; he is, alas, not a prophet, just a would-be torturer and murderer. It is Shakespeare, exploiting the role of Shylock, who slyly provides the material for moral prophecy, which no one in this comedy is prepared or enabled to make.

Shylock, then, is a field of force larger than Shylock himself can encompass, and Shakespeare in *The Merchant of Venice,* as in the later *Measure for Measure,* severely qualifies his comedy by opening onto vistas that comedy rarely can accommodate. Unfortunately, Shakespeare's intimations do not alleviate the savagery of his portrait of the Jew, nor can we suppose they were meant to, for Shakespeare's own audience anyway. The Holocaust made and makes *The Merchant of Venice* unplayable, at least in what appear to be its own terms. With some relief, I turn to

the question of what Shylock did for Shakespeare the poet-
playwright. The surprising answer is that by completing his
emancipation from Marlowe, Shylock made it possible to go on
to *Henry IV, Part One,* with its two characters who surpass even
Shylock in ambivalence: Prince Hal, and the height of Shakespeare's invention of the human, Sir John Falstaff.

Shakespeare's sense of ambivalence is not Freud's, though
clearly Freud, himself so ambivalent about Shakespeare, founds
his account of ambivalence upon materials initially supplied by
Shakespeare. Primal ambivalence, whether in Shakespeare or in
Freud, need not result from social over-determinations. The antipathy between Antonio and Shylock transcends Jew baiting;
Gratiano is an instance of that Christian sport, but Antonio cannot be let off so easily. His ambivalence, like Shylock's, is murderous, and unlike Shylock's, it is successful, for Antonio does
end Shylock the Jew, and gives us Shylock the New Christian.
Freudian ambivalence is simultaneous love and hatred directed
toward the same person; Shakespearean ambivalence, subtler and
more frightening, diverts self-hatred into hatred of the other,
and associates the other with lost possibilities of the self. Hamlet,
whatever his protestations, is truly not interested in revenge, since
no one could be more aware that in revenge all persons blend
into one another. To chop down Claudius is to become old
Hamlet, the ghostly father and not the intellectual prince. It is
horrible to say it, but the broken New Christian Shylock is
preferable to a successful butcher of a Shylock, had Portia not
thwarted him. What would be left for Shylock after hacking up
Antonio? What is left for Antonio after crushing Shylock? In
Shakespearean ambivalence, there can be no victories.

A. P. Rossiter, in his *Angel with Horns* (posthumously published
in 1961), said that ambivalence was peculiarly the dialectic of
Shakespeare's history plays, defining Shakespearean ambivalence as
one mode of irony or another. Irony is indeed so pervasive in

Shakespeare, in every genre, that no comprehensive account of it is possible. What in *The Merchant of Venice* is not ironical, including the Belmont celebration of Act V? The coexistence in Venice of Antonio and of Shylock is an unbearable irony, an ambivalence so acute that it must be ended, either by the barbarous mutilation of Antonio or the barbarous Christian revenge upon Shylock, who evidently is scarcely to be allowed time for instruction before he is baptized. Butchery or baptism is a nice dialectic: the merchant of Venice survives, but the Jew of Venice is immolated, since as a Christian he cannot continue to be a moneylender. Shakespeare's one law is change, and neither Shylock nor Antonio can change. Antonio darkens further and Shylock breaks, but then he is one man against a city.

I end by repeating that it would have been better for the last four centuries of the Jewish people had Shakespeare never written this play. So shadowed and equivocal is *The Merchant Venice,* though, that I cannot be certain that there is any way to perform it now and recover Shakespeare's own art of representing Shylock. Shylock is going to go on making us uncomfortable, enlightened Jew and enlightened Christian, and so I close by wondering if Shylock did not cause Shakespeare more discomfort than we now apprehend. Malvolio is horribly treated, but that appears to be a theatrical in-joke directed against Ben Jonson. Parolles deserves exposure, but the humiliation displayed is withering. Lucio, whose caustic sanity gives us something against which to perspectivize the madnesses of *Measure for Measure,* is compelled by the dubious Duke to marry a whore, for having dared to tell the truth about the Duke of dark corners. Shylock surpasses all these in the outrage visited upon him, and Antonio's turn of the screw, calling for instant conversion, is Shakespeare's own invention, and no part of the pound-of-flesh tradition. Antonio's revenge is one thing, and Shakespeare's quite another. The playwright, capacious soul, would be aware that the gratuitous outrage of a forced conversion to Venetian Christianity surpasses all boundaries of decency. Shylock's revenge upon Shakespeare is that the Jew's dramatic consistency is destroyed when he accepts Christianity rather than death.

Shakespeare thus demeans Shylock, but who can believe Shylock's "I am content"? I remember once observing that Shylock's agreeing to become a Christian is more absurd than would be the conversion of Coriolanus to the popular party, or Cleopatra's consent to become a vestal virgin at Rome. We sooner can see Falstaff as a monk than Shylock as a Christian. Contemplate Shylock at Christian prayer, or confessing to a priest. It will not do; Shakespeare was up to mischief, but you have to be an anti-Semitic scholar, Old Historicist or New, to appreciate fully the ambition of such mischief.

william shakespeare
the merchant of venice

synopsis

Bassanio, a gay, improvident young gentleman of Venice, is very much in love with the beautiful Portia of Belmont, heiress to a princely name and such a colossal fortune that distinguished men from all parts of the world come to court her. Knowing he has no chance of winning her without sufficient funds to defray his expenses, Bassanio turns as usual to his good friend Antonio, a wealthy merchant, regretting his previous heedlessly contracted debts and suggesting that a little present assistance might help him eventually to return all the borrowed money.

The generous, lovable Antonio seems sad, as though vaguely apprehensive of coming distress, but responds immediately to his young friend's request for a loan of three thousand ducats for three months. Antonio's entire wealth at the time happens to be tied up in his merchandise-laden ships at sea, but he breaks his custom of never lending or borrowing on interest and asks Shylock, a rich Jewish money-lender, for the required sum.

The Jew, brooding over insults and injuries and hating the Christian merchant for despising his usurious habits, at once foresees an opportunity for revenge by one desperate act, and blandly agrees to lend the money without interest, provided that Antonio sign a bond, by way of a jest, stipulating that the forfeit be one pound of flesh cut from any part of the body that he, Shylock, may designate. Bassanio protests against taking the loan on such terms, but Antonio dismisses the matter lightly in his confidence that his ships will be back within the next two months, and the gay-hearted lover with his friend, the sportive Gratiano, sets out for Belmont to woo the heiress.

Meanwhile, in her palatial home, Portia is carrying out the terms of her father's will by having each suitor make his choice of three caskets, gold, silver, and lead, the lucky aspirant being the one who will choose the casket containing her picture. With stately ceremony, the Prince of Morocco is led to the caskets and chooses the golden one, only to be disappointed by the picture of a skull. The haughty Prince of Aragon opens the silver one and finds the portrait of an idiot. Then, to Portia's great joy, comes news of Bassanio's arrival, and she orders a song sung during his trial that hints the proper choice. He selects the leaden casket and finding Portia's picture at once claims his bride, who gives him a ring which he vows always to keep.

His friend Gratiano has made love successfully to Portia's confidential companion, the pensive but practical Nerissa, and now another pair appears on the scene, Lorenzo, an artist-friend of Bassanio's, with his bride Jessica, Shylock's pretty daughter, who, bored with the seclusion of her father's house, has eloped with her Christian lover, taking with her in her flight bags of ducats and jewels. They had met Salerio, a messenger, who asked for their company to Belmont where he was ordered to deliver an important letter from Antonio, telling Bassanio that all his ships are lost and he is ruined, that Shylock's forfeit of the pound of flesh from his breast must be paid, and that he greatly desires to see his friend before he dies.

Bassanio is appalled by the tragic news which he explains to Portia, and Salerio adds to his distress by describing the utterly futile efforts that have been made by twenty merchants, the Duke, and prominent Venetian noblemen, to dissuade the Jew from his purpose, even the payment of ten times the amount of the overdue loan having been refused. Hurrying Bassanio through a marriage ceremony, likewise Gratiano and Nerissa, and dispatching the two men to Venice with enough gold to pay Antonio's debt many times over, the level-headed Portia appeals for help to her cousin, a distinguished lawyer, and leaving her household in charge of Lorenzo and Jessica she proceeds to the court in Venice, introduced and disguised as the learned young Doctor Balthasar of Rome, with Nerissa dressed as a lawyer's clerk.

As judge in the case, Portia upholds the law in favor of the Jew who fawns upon her admiringly, but when she makes an eloquent appeal to him to be merciful, Shylock, doubly hardened by the loss of his daughter, his money and jewels, defends himself well and firmly demands the full penalty of the law. This the court awards, but in his moment of triumph as he faces his enemy with whetted knife, the Jew is suddenly warned by Portia, on the pain of death, not to shed a drop of blood or take even a fraction more or less of flesh than the law allows. Adhering strictly to the letter of the law, the young judge then informs the astounded Shylock that, having refused payment of the debt in open court, nothing is due him but his legal forfeiture, and because of his evident plot against the life of a Venetian citizen half of his possessions go to Antonio, the other half to the state, and his life itself lies at the mercy of the Duke alone.

The Duke pardons the broken old man before he can ask, and Antonio requests, while refusing his share, that the Jew make a will leaving his estate at death to his daughter Jessica and her husband. Portia waves aside the fee offered her, but both Nerissa and she for the rings, their own bridal gifts, which Bassanio and Gratiano are wearing. At home again in Belmont, they tease and banter merrily about these trinkets until it is revealed to the amazed men that Portia was the acute doctor of laws and Nerissa her clerk, and Portia hands Antonio a letter telling him of the safe arrival of three of his most valued ships.

historical data

The two romantic stories forming the main plot of *The Merchant of Venice* have appeared separately in the literature of many countries. The story of the caskets is found as early as 800 in the Greek romance *Barlaam and Josaphat* by Joannes Damascenus, and variations are given by the English poet Gower and the Italian novelist Boccaccio. The *Gesta Romanorum*, in the English version by Richard Robinson, *Records of Ancyent Historyes* (1577), contains both this story and that of the pound of flesh. Shakespeare, however, followed more closely the version as presented in *Il Pecorone* by Ser Giovanni Fiorentino (1558) in which not only are both stories combined but "Belmont" is named as the lady's residence.

A play entitled *The Jew*, described by Stephen Gosson in his *School of Abuse* (1579) seems to have combined both plots and another, *The Three Ladies of London* by Robert Wilson (1584), may have suggested the scenes between Antonio and Shylock. Marlowe's *Jew of Malta* is generally conceded to have been of some influence in connection with the relationship of father and daughter.

The play may well have been written in 1594 to take advantage of popular feeling against the Jews stirred up by the conviction of Roderigo Lopez, a Spanish Jew who was physician to Queen Elizabeth and was hanged for plotting her death and that of Antonio Perez, the Portuguese pretender. Some corroboration of this theory may be found in the occurrence of the name Antonio as that of the intended victim in both history and drama.

Scholars are inclined to feel, however, that the maturity and workmanship of the play indicate a later date, and that probably 1596 is the earliest that it was written. Henslowe in his *Diary,* on the other hand, notes the performance of a new play, *The Venesyon Comedy* in 1594, which some commentators insist is the earliest version of *The Merchant.*

In any case the play is listed by Meres in 1598 and entered on the Stationers' Register in that year. Two quarto editions appeared in 1600.

dramatis personæ

The Duke of Venice.

The Prince of Morocco, } *suitors to Portia.*
The Prince of Arragon,

Antonio, *a merchant of Venice.*

Bassanio, *his friend, suitor likewise to Portia.*

Salanio,
Salarino, } *friends to Antonio and Bassanio.*
Gratiano,
Salerio,

Lorenzo, *in love with Jessica.*

Shylock, *a rich Jew.*

Tubal, *a Jew, his friend.*

Launcelot Gobbo, *the clown, servant to Shylock.*

Old Gobbo, *father to Launcelot.*

Leonardo, *servant to Bassanio.*

Balthasar, } *servants to Portia.*
Stephano,

Portia, *a rich heiress.*

Nerissa, *her waiting-maid.*

Jessica, *daughter to Shylock.*

Magnificoes of Venice, Officers of the Court of Justice, Gaoler, Servants to Portia, and other Attendants.

Scene: Partly at Venice, and partly at Belmont, the seat of Portia, on the Continent

act 1

scene 1. [*Venice; A street*]

Enter Antonio, Salarino, *and* Salanio

Antonio. In sooth, I know not why I am so sad:
    It wearies me, you say it wearies you;
    But how I caught it, found it, or came by it,
    What stuff 'tis made of, whereof it is born,
    I am to learn,
    And such a want-wit sadness makes of me,
    That I have much ado to know myself.

Salarino. Your mind is tossing on the ocean,
    There where your argosies with portly sail
    Like signiors and rich burghers on the flood,
    Or, as it were, the pageants of the sea,
    Do overpeer the petty traffickers
    That curt'sy to them, do them reverence,
    As they fly by them with their woven wings.

Salanio. Believe me, sir, had I such venture forth,
    The better part of my affections would
    Be with my hopes abroad. I should be still

Plucking the grass, to know where sits the wind,
Peering in maps for ports, and piers, and roads;
And every object that might make me fear
Misfortune to my ventures, out of doubt
Would make me sad.

Salarino.   My wind, cooling my broth,
Would blow me to an ague, when I thought
What harm a wind too great at sea might do.
I should not see the sandy hour-glass run,
But I should think of shallows and of flats,
And see my wealthy Andrew dock'd in sand
Vailing her high top lower than her ribs
To kiss her burial. Should I go to church
And see the holy edifice of stone,
And not bethink me straight of dangerous rocks,
Which touching but my gentle vessel's side
Would scatter all her spices on the stream,
Enrobe the roaring waters with my silks;
And in a word, but even now worth this,
And now worth nothing? Shall I have the thought
To think on this, and shall I lack the thought
That such a thing bechanced would make me sad?
But tell not me; I know Antonio
Is sad to think upon his merchandise.

Antonio. Believe me, no: I thank my fortune for it,
My ventures are not in one bottom trusted,
Nor to one place; nor is my whole estate
Upon the fortune of this present year:
Therefore my merchandise makes me not sad.

Salarino. Why, then you are in love.

Antonio.   Fie, fie!

Salarino. Not in love neither? Then let us say you are sad
    Because you are not merry: and 'twere as easy
    For you to laugh, and leap, and say you are merry
    Because you are not sad. Now, by two-headed Janus,
    Nature hath framed strange fellows in her time:
    Some that will evermore peep through their eyes,
    And laugh like parrots at a bag-piper;
    And other of such vinegar aspect,
    That they'll not show their teeth in way of smile,
    Though Nestor swear the jest be laughable.

            Enter Bassanio, Lorenzo, *and* Gratiano

Salanio. Here comes Bassanio, your most noble kinsman,
    Gratiano, and Lorenzo. Fare ye well:
    We leave you now with better company.

Salarino. I would have stay'd till I had made you merry,
    If worthier friends had not prevented me.

Antonio. Your worth is very dear in my regard.
    I take it, your own business calls on you,
    And you embrace th' occasion to depart.

Salarino. Good morrow, my good lords.

Bassanio. Good signiors both, when shall we laugh? say, when?
    You grow exceeding strange: must it be so?

Salarino. We'll make our leisures to attend on yours.

            Exeunt Salarino *and* Salanio.

Lorenzo. My Lord Bassanio, since you have found Antonio,
    We two will leave you: but at dinner-time
    I pray you have in mind where we must meet.

Bassanio. I will not fail you.

Gratiano. You look not well, Signior Antonio,
    You have too much respect upon the world:

They lose it that do buy it with much care.
Believe me, you are marvellously changed.

Antonio. I hold the world but as the world, Gratiano,
A stage, where every man must play a part,
And mine a sad one.

Gratiano.   Let me play the fool:
With mirth and laughter let old wrinkles come,
And let my liver rather heat with wine
Than my heart cool with mortifying groans.
Why should a man, whose blood is warm within,
Sit like his grandsire cut in alabaster?
Sleep when he wakes, and creep into the jaundice
By being peevish? I tell thee what, Antonio—
I love thee, and it is my love that speaks—
There are a sort of men, whose visages
Do cream and mantle like a standing pond,
And do a wilful stillness entertain,
With purpose to be dress'd in an opinion
Of wisdom, gravity, profound conceit,
As who should say, 'I am Sir Oracle,
And, when I ope my lips, let no dog bark!'
O my Antonio, I do know of these
That therefore only are reputed wise
For saying nothing; when I am very sure
If they should speak, would almost damn those ears
Which, hearing them, would call their brothers fools.
I'll tell thee more of this another time:
But fish not with this melancholy bait
For this fool gudgeon, this opinion.
Come, good Lorenzo. Fare ye well awhile:
I'll end my exhortation after dinner.

Lorenzo. Well, we will leave you, then, till dinner-time:
    I must be one of these same dumb wise men,
    For Gratiano never lets me speak.

Gratiano. Well, keep me company but two years moe,
    Thou shalt not know the sound of thine own tongue.

Antonio. Farewell: I'll grow a talker for this gear.

Gratiano. Thanks, i'faith; for silence is only commendable
    In a neat's tongue dried, and a maid not vendible.

                     Exeunt Gratiano *and* Lorenzo.

Antonio. Is that anything now?

Bassanio. Gratiano speaks an infinite deal of nothing, more than
    any man in all Venice. His reasons are as two grains of wheat
    hid in two bushels of chaff: you shall seek all day ere you find
    them; and when you have them, they are not worth the search.

Antonio. Well, tell me now, what lady is the same
    To whom you swore a secret pilgrimage,
    That you today promised to tell me of?

Bassanio. 'Tis not unknown to you, Antonio,
    How much I have disabled mine estate,
    By something showing a more swelling port
    Than my faint means would grant continuance:
    Nor do I now make moan to be abridged
    From such a noble rate, but my chief care
    Is to come fairly off from the great debts
    Wherein my time, something too prodigal,
    Hath left me gaged. To you, Antonio,
    I owe the most in money and in love,
    And from your love I have a warranty
    To unburthen all my plots and purposes
    How to get clear of all the debts I owe.

Antonio. I pray you, good Bassanio, let me know it,
And if it stand, as you yourself still do,
Within the eye of honour, be assured
My purse, my person, my extremest means
Lie all unlock'd to your occasions.

Bassanio. In my school-days, when I had lost one shaft,
I shot his fellow of the self-same flight
The self-same way with more advised watch
To find the other forth, and by adventuring both,
I oft found both: I urge this childhood proof
Because what follows is pure innocence.
I owe you much and, like a wilful youth,
That which I owe is lost, but if you please
To shoot another arrow that self way
Which you did shoot the first, I do not doubt,
As I will watch the aim, or to find both
Or bring your latter hazard back again,
And thankfully rest debtor for the first.

Antonio. You know me well, and herein spend but time
To wind about my love with circumstance,
And out of doubt you do me now more wrong
In making question of my uttermost,
Than if you had made waste of all I have:
Then do but say to me what I should do
That in your knowledge may by me be done,
And I am prest unto it: therefore, speak.

Bassanio. In Belmont is a lady richly left;
And she is fair and, fairer than that word,
Of wondrous virtues: sometimes from her eyes
I did receive fair speechless messages:
Her name is Portia, nothing undervalued

To Cato's daughter, Brutus' Portia,
Nor is the wide world ignorant of her worth,
For the four winds blow in from every coast
Renowned suitors, and her sunny locks
Hang on her temples like a golden fleece,
Which makes her seat of Belmont Colchos' strond,
And many Jasons come in quest of her.
O my Antonio, had I but the means
To hold a rival place with one of them,
I have a mind presages me such thrift,
That I should questionless be fortunate!

Antonio. Thou know'st that all my fortunes are at sea;
Neither have I money, nor commodity
To raise a present sum: therefore go forth,
Try what my credit can in Venice do—
That shall be rack'd, even to the uttermost
To furnish thee to Belmont, to fair Portia.
Go presently inquire, and so will I,
Where money is, and I no question make
To have it of my trust, or for my sake.

Exeunt.

scene 2. *[Belmont; A room in* Portia's *house]*

Enter Portia *and* Nerissa

Portia. By my troth, Nerissa, my little body is aweary of this great world.

Nerissa. You would be, sweet madam, if your miseries were in the same abundance as your good fortunes are: and yet for aught I see, they are as sick that surfeit with too much, as they that starve with nothing. It is no mean happiness, therefore, to be seated in the mean: superfluity comes sooner by white hairs, but competency lives longer.

Portia. Good sentences, and well pronounced.

Nerissa. They would be better if well followed.

Portia. If to do were as easy as to know what were good to do, chapels had been churches, and poor men's cottages princes' palaces. It is a good divine that follows his own instructions: I can easier teach twenty what were good to be done, than be one of the twenty to follow mine own teaching. The brain may devise laws for the blood, but a hot temper leaps o'er a cold decree: such a hare is madness the youth, to skip o'er the meshes of good counsel the cripple. But this reasoning is not in the fashion to choose me a husband. O me, the word 'choose'! I may neither choose whom I would, nor refuse whom I dislike; so is the will of a living daughter curbed by the will of a dead father. Is it not hard, Nerissa, that I cannot choose one, nor refuse none?

Nerissa. Your father was ever virtuous, and holy men at their death have good inspirations: therefore the lottery that he hath devised in these three chests of gold, silver, and lead— whereof who chooses his meaning chooses you—will no doubt never be chosen by any rightly, but one who shall rightly love. But what warmth is there in your affection towards any of these princely suitors that are already come?

Portia. I pray thee, over-name them, and as thou namest them, I will describe them, and according to my description, level at my affection.

Nerissa. First, there is the Neapolitan prince.

Portia. Ay, that's a colt indeed, for he doth nothing but talk of his horse, and he makes it a great appropriation to his own

good parts that he can shoe him himself. I am much afeard
my lady his mother played false with a smith.

Nerissa. Then there is the County Palatine.

Portia. He doth nothing but frown 'as who should say, 'if you
will not have me, choose' he hears merry tales, and smiles
not: I fear he will prove the weeping philosopher when he
grows old, being so full of unmannerly sadness in his youth.
I had rather be married to a death's-head with a bone in
his mouth than to either of these. God defend me from
these two!

Nerissa. How say you by the French lord, Monsieur Le Bon?

Portia. God made him, and therefore let him pass for a man. In
truth, I know it is a sin to be a mocker, but he!—why, he
hath a horse better than the Neapolitan's; a better bad habit
of frowning than the Count Palatine: he is every man in no
man; if a throstle sing, he falls straight a capering: he will
fence with his own shadow. If I should marry him, I should
marry twenty husbands. If he would despise me, I would
forgive him, for if he love me to madness, I shall never
requite him.

Nerissa. What say you, then, to Falconbridge, the young baron
of England?

Portia. You know I say nothing to him, for he understands not
me, nor I him: he hath neither Latin, French, nor Italian, and
you will come into the court and swear that I have a poor
pennyworth in the English. He is a proper man's picture, but
alas, who can converse with a dumb-show? How oddly he is
suited! I think he bought his doublet in Italy, his round hose
in France, his bonnet in Germany, and his behaviour
everywhere.

Nerissa. What think you of the Scottish lord, his neighbour?

Portia. That he hath a neighbourly charity in him, for he borrowed a box of the ear of the Englishman, and swore he would pay him again when he was able: I think the Frenchman became his surety, and sealed under for another.

Nerissa. How like you the young German, the Duke of Saxony's nephew?

Portia. Very vilely in the morning when he is sober, and most vilely in the afternoon, when he is drunk: when he is best, he is a little worse than a man; and when he is worst, he is little better than a beast. An the worst fall that ever fell, I hope I shall make shift to go without him.

Nerissa. If he should offer to choose, and choose the right casket, you should refuse to perform your father's will, if you should refuse to accept him.

Portia. Therefore, for fear of the worst, I pray thee set a deep glass of Rhenish wine on the contrary casket, for, if the devil be within and that temptation without, I know he will choose it. I will do anything, Nerissa, ere I'll be married to a sponge.

Nerissa. You need not fear, lady, the having any of these lords: they have acquainted me with their determinations, which is indeed to return to their home, and to trouble you with no more suit, unless you may be won by some other sort than your father's imposition, depending on the caskets.

Portia. If I live to be as old as Sibylla, I will die as chaste as Diana, unless I be obtained by the manner of my father's will. I am glad this parcel of wooers are so reasonable, for there is not one among them but I dote on his very absence; and I pray God grant them a fair departure.

Nerissa. Do you not remember, lady, in your father's time, a Venetian, a scholar, and a soldier, that came hither in company of the Marquis of Montferrat?

Portia. Yes, yes, it was Bassanio, as I think he was so called.

Nerissa. True, madam: he, of all the men that ever my foolish eyes looked upon, was the best deserving a fair lady.

Portia. I remember him well, and I remember him worthy of thy praise.

Enter a Serving-man

How now, what news?

Serving-man. The four strangers seek for you, madam, to take their leave: and there is a forerunner come from a fifth, the Prince of Morocco, who brings word the prince his master will be here tonight.

Portia. If I could bid the fifth welcome with so good a heart as I can bid the other four farewell, I should be glad of his approach: if he have the condition of a saint and the complexion of a devil, I had rather he should shrive me than wive me.
Come, Nerissa. Sirrah, go before.
Whiles we shut the gates upon one wooer, another knocks at the door.

Exeunt.

scene 3. [*Venice; A public place*]

Enter Bassanio *and* Shylock

Shylock. Three thousand ducats, well.

Bassanio. Ay, sir, for three months.

Shylock. For three months, well.

Bassanio. For the which, as I told you, Antonio shall be bound.

Shylock. Antonio shall become bound; well.

Bassanio. May you stead me? Will you pleasure me? Shall I know your answer?

Shylock. Three thousand ducats for three months, and Antonio bound.

Bassanio. Your answer to that.

Shylock. Antonio is a good man.

Bassanio. Have you heard any imputation to the contrary?

Shylock. Ho, no, no, no, no: my meaning in saying he is a good man, is to have you understand me that he is sufficient. Yet his means are in supposition: he hath an argosy bound to Tripolis, another to the Indies; I understand moreover upon the Rialto, he hath a third at Mexico, a fourth for England, and other ventures he hath squandered abroad. But ships are but boards, sailors but men: there be land-rats and water-rats, water-thieves and land-thieves, I mean pirates; and then there is the peril of waters, winds, and rocks. The man is notwithstanding sufficient. Three thousand ducats—I think I may take his bond.

Bassanio. Be assured you may.

Shylock. I will be assured I may, and that I may be assured, I will bethink me. May I speak with Antonio?

Bassanio. If it please you to dine with us.

Shylock. Yes, to smell pork, to eat of the habitation which your prophet the Nazarite conjured the devil into. I will buy with you, sell with you, talk with you, walk with you, and so following: but I will not eat with you, drink with you, nor pray with you. What news on the Rialto? Who is he comes here?

Enter Antonio

Bassanio. This is Signior Antonio.

Shylock. [*Aside*] How like a fawning publican he looks!
   I hate him for he is a Christian;
   But more for that in low simplicity
   He lends out money gratis and brings down
   The rate of usance here with us in Venice.
   If I can catch him once upon the hip,
   I will feed fat the ancient grudge I bear him.
   He hates our sacred nation, and he rails,
   Even there where merchants most do congregate,
   On me, my bargains, and my well-won thrift,
   Which he calls interest. Cursed be my tribe
   If I forgive him!

Bassanio.   Shylock, do you hear?

Shylock. I am debating of my present store,
   And, by the near guess of my memory,
   I cannot instantly raise up the gross
   Of full three thousand ducats. What of that?
   Tubal, a wealthy Hebrew of my tribe,
   Will furnish me. But soft! How many months
   Do you desire? [*to Antonio*] Rest you fair, good signior;
   Your worship was the last man in our mouths.

Antonio. Shylock, although I neither lend nor borrow
   By taking nor by giving of excess,
   Yet to supply the ripe wants of my friend,
   I'll break a custom. [*To Bassanio*] Is he yet possess'd
   How much ye would?

Shylock.   Ay, ay, three thousand ducats.

Antonio. And for three months.

Shylock. I had forgot; three months, you told me so.
   Well then, your bond: and let me see; but hear you;
   Methought you said you neither lend nor borrow
   Upon advantage.

Antonio.   I do never use it.

Shylock. When Jacob grazed his uncle Laban's sheep—
   This Jacob from our holy Abram was,
   As his wise mother wrought in his behalf,
   The third possessor; ay, he was the third—

Antonio. And what of him? Did he take interest?

Shylock. No, not take interest; not, as you would say,
   Directly interest: mark what Jacob did.
   When Laban and himself were compromised
   That all the eanlings which were streak'd and pied
   Should fall as Jacob's hire, the ewes being rank
   In the end of Autumn turned to the rams,
   And when the work of generation was
   Between these woolly breeders in the act,
   The skilful shepherd peel'd me certain wands,
   And, in the doing of the deed of kind,
   He stuck them up before the fulsome ewes,
   Who then conceiving, did in eaning time
   Fall parti-colour'd lambs, and those were Jacob's.
   This was a way to thrive, and he was blest:
   And thrift is blessing if men steal it not.

Antonio. This was a venture, sir, that Jacob served for,
   A thing not in his power to bring to pass,
   But sway'd and fashion'd by the hand of heaven.
   Was this inserted to make interest good?
   Or is your gold and silver ewes and rams?

Shylock. I cannot tell, I make it breed as fast—
   But note me, signior.

Antonio.   Mark you this, Bassanio,
   The devil can cite Scripture for his purpose.
   An evil soul producing holy witness

Is like a villain with a smiling cheek;
A goodly apple rotten at the heart:
O, what a goodly outside falsehood hath!

Shylock. Three thousand ducats; 'tis a good round sum.
Three months from twelve; then let me see the rate—

Antonio. Well, Shylock, shall we be beholding to you?

Shylock. Signior Antonio, many a time and oft
In the Rialto you have rated me
About my moneys and my usances:
Still have I borne it with a patient shrug,
For sufferance is the badge of all our tribe.
You call me misbeliever, cut-throat dog,
And spit upon my Jewish gaberdine,
And all for use of that which is mine own.
Well then, it now appears you need my help:
Go to, then; you come to me, and you say
'Shylock, we would have moneys,' you say so;
You, that did void your rheum upon my beard,
And foot me as you spurn a stranger cur
Over your threshold: moneys is your suit.
What should I say to you? Should I not say
'Hath a dog money? Is it possible
A cur can lend three thousand ducats?' or
Shall I bend low and in a bondman's key,
With bated breath and whispering humbleness,
Say this—
'Fair sir, you spit on me on Wednesday last,
You spurn'd me such a day, another time
You call'd me dog; and for these courtesies
I'll lend you thus much moneys'?

Antonio. I am as like to call thee so again,
To spit on thee again, to spurn thee too.

If thou wilt lend this money, lend it not
As to thy friends, for when did friendship take
A breed for barren metal of his friend?
But lend it rather to thine enemy,
Who if he break, thou mayst with better face
Exact the penalty.

Shylock.　　　　　　Why, look you how you storm!
　I would be friends with you, and have your love,
Forget the shames that you have stain'd me with,
Supply your present wants, and take no doit
Of usance for my moneys, and you'll not hear me—
This is kind I offer.

Bassanio. This were kindness.

Shylock.　　　　　　This kindness will I show.
Go with me to a notary, seal me there
Your single bond; and, in a merry sport,
If you repay me not on such a day,
In such a place, such sum or sums as are
Express'd in the condition, let the forfeit
Be nominated for an equal pound
Of your fair flesh, to be cut off and taken
In what part of your body pleaseth me.

Antonio. Content, i' faith: I'll seal to such a bond,
And say there is much kindness in the Jew.

Bassanio. You shall not seal to such a bond for me:
I'll rather dwell in my necessity.

Antonio. Why fear not, man; I will not forfeit it.
Within these two months, that's a month before
This bond expires, I do expect return
Of thrice three times the value of this bond.

Shylock. O father Abram, what these Christians are,
Whose own hard dealings teaches them suspect
The thoughts of others! Pray you, tell me this;
If he should break his day, what should I gain
By the exaction of the forfeiture?
A pound of man's flesh taken from a man
Is not so estimable, profitable neither
As flesh of muttons, beefs, or goats. I say,
To buy his favour, I extend this friendship:
If he will take it, so; if not, adieu,
And, for my love, I pray you wrong me not.

Antonio. Yes, Shylock, I will seal unto this bond.

Shylock. Then meet me forthwith at the notary's,
Give him direction for this merry bond,
And I will go and purse the ducats straight,
See to my house, left in the fearful guard
Of an unthrifty knave; and presently
I will be with you.

Antonio.   Hie thee, gentle Jew.

                                        Exit Shylock.

The Hebrew will turn Christian: he grows kind.

Bassanio. I like not fair terms and a villain's mind.

Antonio. Come on, in this there can be no dismay;
My ships come home a month before the day.

                                        Exeunt.

act 2

scene 1. [*Belmont; A room in* Portia's *house*]

Flourish of cornets. Enter the Prince of Morocco *and his train;*
Portia, Nerissa, *and others attending*

Prince of Morocco. Mislike me not for my complexion,
The shadow'd livery of the burnish'd sun,
To whom I am a neighbour and near bred.
Bring me the fairest creature northward born,
Where Phœbus' fire scarce thaws the icicles,
And let us make incision for your love,
To prove whose blood is reddest, his or mine.
I tell thee, lady, this aspect of mine
Hath fear'd the valiant—by my love, I swear
The best-regarded virgins of our clime
Have loved it too: I would not change this hue,
Except to steal your thoughts, my gentle queen.

Portia. In terms of choice I am not solely led
By nice direction of a maiden's eyes;
Besides, the lottery of my destiny

Bars me the right of voluntary choosing:
But if my father had not scanted me
And hedged me by his wit, to yield myself
His wife who wins me by that means I told you,
Yourself, renowned prince, then stood as fair
As any comer I have look'd on yet
For my affection.

Prince of Morocco.   Even for that I thank you:
Therefore, I pray you, lead me to the caskets
To try my fortune. By this scimitar
That slew the Sophy and a Persian prince
That won three fields of Sultan Solyman,
I would outstare the sternest eyes that look,
Outbrave the heart most daring on the earth,
Pluck the young sucking cubs from the she-bear,
Yea, mock the lion when he roars for prey,
To win thee, lady. But alas the while!
If Hercules and Lichas play at dice
Which is the better man, the greater throw
May turn by fortune from the weaker hand:
So is Alcides beaten by his rage,
And so may I, blind fortune leading me,
Miss that which one unworthier may attain,
And die with grieving.

Portia.   You must take your chance,
And either not attempt to choose at all,
Or swear before you choose, if you choose wrong
Never to speak to lady afterward
In way of marriage: therefore be advised.

Prince of Morocco. Nor will not. Come, bring me unto my
chance.

Portia. First, forward to the temple: after dinner
 Your hazard shall be made.

Prince of Morocco.   Good fortune then!
 To make me blest or cursed'st among men.

                                        Cornets, and exeunt.

scene 2.   [*Venice; A street*]

Enter Launcelot

Launcelot. Certainly my conscience will serve me to run from
 this Jew my master. The fiend is at mine elbow, and tempts
 me, saying to me, 'Gobbo, Launcelot Gobbo, good
 Launcelot,' or 'good Gobbo,' or 'good Launcelot Gobbo, use
 your legs, take the start, run away.' My conscience says, 'No;
 take heed, honest Launcelot; take heed, honest Gobbo,' or
 as aforesaid, 'honest Launcelot Gobbo, do not run, scorn
 running with thy heels.' Well, the most courageous fiend bids
 me pack: 'Fia!' says the fiend, 'away!' says the fiend, 'for the
 heavens, rouse up a brave mind,' says the fiend, 'and run.'
 Well, my conscience, hanging about the neck of my heart,
 says very wisely to me, 'My honest friend Launcelot, being
 an honest man's son—or rather an honest woman's son—for,
 indeed my father did something smack, something grow to,
 he had a kind of taste;—well, my conscience says, 'Launcelot,
 budge not.' 'Budge,' says the fiend. 'Budge not,' says my
 conscience. 'Conscience,' say I, 'you counsel well;' 'Fiend,'
 say I, 'you counsel well:' to be ruled by my conscience, I
 should stay with the Jew my master, who, God bless the
 mark, is a kind of devil; and to run away from the Jew, I
 should be ruled by the fiend, who, saving your reverence, is
 the devil himself. Certainly the Jew is the very devil incarnal;
 and in my conscience, my conscience is but a kind of hard

conscience, to offer to counsel me to stay with the Jew. The fiend gives the more friendly counsel: I will run, fiend, my heels are at your command; I will run.

Enter Old Gobbo, *with a basket*

Gobbo. Master young man, you, I pray you, which is the way to master Jew's?

Launcelot. [*Aside*] O heavens, this is my true-begotten father! Who being more than sand-blind, high-gravel blind, knows me not: I will try confusions with him.

Gobbo. Master young gentleman, I pray you, which is the way to master Jew's?

Launcelot. Turn up on your right hand at the next turning, but at the next turning of all, on your left; marry, at the very next turning turn of no hand, but turn down indirectly to the Jew's house.

Gobbo. By God's sonties, 'twill be a hard way to hit. Can you tell me whether one Launcelot that dwells with him, dwell with him or no?

Launcelot. Talk you of young Master Launcelot? [*Aside*] Mark me now, now will I raise the waters. Talk you of young Master Launcelot?

Gobbo. No master, sir, but a poor man's son: his father, though I say it, is an honest exceeding poor man, and, God be thanked, well to live.

Launcelot. Well, let his father be what a' will, we talk of young Master Launcelot.

Gobbo. Your worship's friend, and Launcelot, sir.

Launcelot. But I pray you, ergo old man, ergo I beseech you, talk you of young Master Launcelot?

Gobbo. Of Launcelot, an't please your mastership.

Launcelot. Ergo Master Launcelot. Talk not of Master Launcelot, father, for the young gentleman, according to Fates and Destinies and such odd sayings, the Sisters Three and such branches of learning, is indeed deceased, or as you would say in plain terms, gone to heaven.

Gobbo. Marry, God forbid! The boy was the very staff of my age, my very prop.

Launcelot. Do I look like a cudgel or a hovel-post, a staff or a prop? Do you know me, father?

Gobbo. Alack the day, I know you not, young gentleman, but I pray you tell me, is my boy, God rest his soul, alive or dead?

Launcelot. Do you not know me, father?

Gobbo. Alack sir, I am sand-blind, I know you not.

Launcelot. Nay, indeed if you had your eyes, you might fail of the knowing me: it is a wise father that knows his own child. Well, old man, I will tell you news of your son—give me your blessing: truth will come to light, murder cannot be hid long, a man's son may, but at the length, truth will out.

Gobbo. Pray you, sir, stand up: I am sure you are not Launcelot, my boy.

Launcelot. Pray you, let's have no more fooling about it, but give me your blessing: I am Launcelot, your boy that was, your son that is, your child that shall be.

Gobbo. I cannot think you are my son.

Launcelot. I know not what I shall think of that: but I am Launcelot, the Jew's man, and I am sure Margery your wife is my mother.

Gobbo. Her name is Margery, indeed: I'll be sworn if thou be Launcelot, thou art mine own flesh and blood. Lord worshipped might he be! What a beard hast thou got! Thou hast got more hair on thy chin than Dobbin my fill-horse has on his tail.

Launcelot. It should seem, then, that Dobbin's tail grows backward: I am sure he had more hair of his tail than I have of my face when I last saw him.

Gobbo. Lord, how art thou changed! How dost thou and thy master agree? I have brought him a present. How 'gree you now?

Launcelot. Well, well, but for mine own part, as I have set up my rest to run away, so I will not rest till I have run some ground. My master's a very Jew: give him a present! Give him a halter: I am famished in his service. You may tell every finger I have with my ribs. Father, I am glad you are come: give me your present to one Master Bassanio, who indeed gives rare new liveries: if I serve not him, I will run as far as God has any ground. O rare fortune! Here comes the man: to him, father, for I am a Jew if I serve the Jew any longer.

Enter Bassanio, *with* Leonardo *and other followers*

Bassanio. You may do so, but let it be so hasted that supper be ready at the farthest by five of the clock. See these letters delivered, put the liveries to making, and desire Gratiano to come anon to my lodging.

Exit a Servant.

Launcelot. To him, father.

Gobbo. God bless your worship!

Bassanio. Gramercy, wouldst thou aught with me?

Gobbo. Here's my son, sir, a poor boy,—

Launcelot. Not a poor boy, sir, but the rich Jew's man that would, sir,—as my father shall specify—

Gobbo. He hath a great infection, sir, as one would say, to serve—

Launcelot. Indeed, the short and the long is, I serve the Jew, and have a desire—as my father shall specify—

Gobbo. His master and he, saving your worship's reverence, are scarce cater-cousins,—

Launcelot. To be brief, the very truth is that the Jew having done me wrong, doth cause me—as my father, being I hope an old man, shall frutify unto you—

Gobbo. I have here a dish of doves that I would bestow upon your worship, and my suit is—

Launcelot. In very brief, the suit is impertinent to myself, as your worship shall know by this honest old man, and though I say it, though old man, yet poor man, my father.

Bassanio. One speak for both. What would you?

Launcelot. Serve you, sir.

Gobbo. That is the very defect of the matter, sir.

Bassanio. I know thee well; thou hast obtain'd thy suit:
Shylock thy master spoke with me this day,
And hath preferr'd thee, if it be preferment
To leave a rich Jew's service, to become
The follower of so poor a gentleman.

Launcelot. The old proverb is very well parted between my master Shylock and you, sir: you have the 'grace of God,' sir, and he hath 'enough.'

Bassanio. Thou speak'st it well. Go, father, with thy son.
Take leave of thy old master and inquire
My lodging out. [*To followers*] Give him a livery
More guarded than his fellows': see it done.

Launcelot. Father, in. I cannot get a service, no! I have ne'er a tongue in my head. Well, if any man in Italy have a fairer table which doth offer to swear upon a book, I shall have good fortune. Go to, here's a simple line of life, here's a small trifle of wives: alas, fifteen wives is nothing! a'leven widows and nine maids is a simple coming-in for one man, and then to 'scape drowning thrice, and to be in peril of my life with the edge of a feather-bed, here are simple scapes. Well, if Fortune be a woman she's a good wench for this gear. Father, come; I'll take my leave of the Jew in the twinkling of an eye.

Exeunt Launcelot *and* Old Gobbo.

Bassanio. I pray thee, good Leonardo, think on this:
These things being bought and orderly bestow'd,
Return in haste, for I do feast tonight
My best-esteem'd acquaintance: hie thee, go.

Leonardo. My best endeavours shall be done herein.

Enter Gratiano

Gratiano. Where is your master?

Leonardo.   Yonder, sir, he walks.

Exit.

Gratiano. Signior Bassanio—

Bassanio. Gratiano!

Gratiano. I have a suit to you.

Bassanio.   You have obtain'd it.

Gratiano. You must not deny me: I must go with you to Belmont.

Bassanio. Why then you must. But hear thee, Gratiano:
Thou art too wild, too rude, and bold of voice;
Parts that become thee happily enough,
And in such eyes as ours appear not faults;
But where thou art not known, why there they show

Something too liberal. Pray thee, take pain
To allay with some cold drops of modesty
Thy skipping spirit, lest through thy wild behaviour
I be misconstrued in the place I go to,
And lose my hopes.

Gratiano.   Signior Bassanio, hear me:
If I do not put on a sober habit,
Talk with respect, and swear but now and then,
Wear prayer-books in my pocket, look demurely,
Nay more, while grace is saying; hood mine eyes
Thus with my hat, and sigh and say 'amen';
Use all the observance of civility,
Like one well studied in a sad ostent
To please his grandam, never trust me more.

Bassanio. Well, we shall see your bearing.

Gratiano. Nay, but I bar tonight: you shall not gauge me
By what we do tonight.

Bassanio.   No, that were pity:
I would entreat you rather to put on
Your boldest suit of mirth, for we have friends
That purpose merriment. But fare you well,
I have some business.

Gratiano. And I must to Lorenzo and the rest,
But we will visit you at supper-time.

Exeunt.

scene 3.   [*The same; A room in* Shylock's *house*]

Enter Jessica *and* Launcelot

Jessica. I am sorry thou wilt leave my father so.
Our house is hell; and thou, a merry devil,

Didst rob it of some taste of tediousness.
But fare thee well; there is a ducat for thee,
And Launcelot, soon at supper shalt thou see
Lorenzo, who is thy new master's guest:
Give him this letter—do it secretly—
And so farewell: I would not have my father
See me in talk with thee.

Launcelot. Adieu! Tears exhibit my tongue. Most beautiful
pagan, most sweet Jew! If a Christian did not play the knave
and get thee, I am much deceived. But adieu, these foolish
drops do something drown my manly spirit: adieu.

Jessica. Farewell, good Launcelot.

Exit Launcelot.

Alack, what heinous sin is it in me
To be ashamed to be my father's child!
But though I am a daughter to his blood,
I am not to his manners. O Lorenzo,
If thou keep promise, I shall end this strife,
Become a Christian and thy loving wife.

Exit.

scene 4. [*The same; A street*]

Enter Gratiano, Lorenzo, Salarino, *and* Salanio

Lorenzo. Nay, we will slink away in supper-time,
  Disguise us at my lodging, and return
  All in an hour.

Gratiano. We have not made good preparation.

Salarino. We have not spoke us yet of torch-bearers.

Salanio. 'Tis vile unless it may be quaintly order'd,
  And better in my mind not undertook.

Lorenzo. 'Tis now but four o'clock: we have two hours
    To furnish us.

                      Enter Launcelot, *with a letter*
                  Friend Launcelot, what's the news?

Launcelot. An it shall please you to break up this, it shall seem to
    signify.

Lorenzo. I know the hand, in faith 'tis a fair hand,
    And whiter than the paper it writ on
    Is the fair hand that writ.

Gratiano.   Love-news, in faith.

Launcelot. By your leave, sir.

Lorenzo. Whither goest thou?

Launcelot. Marry sir, to bid my old master the Jew to sup
    tonight with my new master the Christian.

Lorenzo. Hold here, take this: tell gentle Jessica
    I will not fail her; speak it privately.
    Go, gentlemen,

                            Exit Launcelot.
    Will you prepare you for this masque tonight?
    I am provided of a torch-bearer.

Salarino. Ay marry, I'll be gone about it straight.

Salanio. And so will I.

Lorenzo.   Meet me and Gratiano
    At Gratiano's lodging some hour hence.

Salarino. 'Tis good we do so.

                 Exeunt Salarino *and* Salanio.

Gratiano. Was not that letter from fair Jessica?

Lorenzo. I must needs tell thee all. She hath directed
    How I shall take her from her father's house,
    What gold and jewels she is furnish'd with,

What page's suit she hath in readiness.
If e'er the Jew her father come to heaven,
It will be for his gentle daughter's sake:
And never dare misfortune cross her foot
Unless she do it under this excuse,
That she is issue to a faithless Jew.
Come, go with me, peruse this as thou goest:
Fair Jessica shall be my torch-bearer.

Exeunt.

scene 5. [*The same; Before* Shylock's *house*]

Enter Shylock *and* Launcelot

Shylock. Well, thou shalt see, thy eyes shall be thy judge,
The difference of old Shylock and Bassanio:—
What, Jessica!—thou shalt not gormandise
As thou hast done with me:—What, Jessica!—
And sleep and snore, and rend apparel out;—
Why, Jessica, I say!

Launcelot.   Why, Jessica!

Shylock. Who bids thee call? I do not bid thee call.

Launcelot. Your worship was wont to tell me that I could do
nothing without bidding.

Enter Jessica

Jessica. Call you? What is your will?

Shylock. I am bid forth to supper, Jessica:
There are my keys. But wherefore should I go?
I am not bid for love; they flatter me,
But yet I'll go in hate, to feed upon
The prodigal Christian. Jessica my girl,
Look to my house. I am right loath to go:

There is some ill a-brewing towards my rest,
For I did dream of money-bags tonight.

Launcelot. I beseech you, sir, go: my young master doth expect
your reproach.

Shylock. So do I his.

Launcelot. And they have conspired together, I will not say you
shall see a masque, but if you do, then it was not for nothing
that my nose fell a-bleeding on Black–Monday last at six
o'clock i' the morning, falling out that year on Ash–
Wednesday was four year, in the afternoon.

Shylock. What, are there masques? Hear you me, Jessica:
Lock up my doors, and when you hear the drum
And the vile squealing of the wry-neck'd fife,
Clamber not you up to the casements then,
Nor thrust your head into the public street
To gaze on Christian fools with varnish'd faces;
But stop my house's ears, I mean my casements,
Let not the sound of shallow foppery enter
My sober house. By Jacob's staff, I swear
I have no mind of feasting forth tonight:
But I will go. Go you before me, sirrah,
Say I will come.

Launcelot. I will go before, sir. Mistress, look out at window,
for all this—
There will come a Christian by,
Will be worth a Jewes' eye.

Exit.

Shylock. What says that fool of Hagar's offspring, ha?

Jessica. His words were 'Farewell, mistress,' nothing else.

Shylock. The patch is kind enough, but a huge feeder,
Snail-slow in profit, and he sleeps by day

More than the wild-cat: drones hive not with me,
Therefore I part with him, and part with him
To one that I would have him help to waste
His borrow'd purse. Well, Jessica, go in.
Perhaps I will return immediately:
Do as I bid you, shut doors after you,
Fast bind, fast find,
A proverb never stale in thrifty mind.

Exit.

Jessica. Farewell; and if my fortune be not crost,
I have a father, you a daughter, lost.

Exit.

scene 6. [*The same*]

Enter Gratiano *and* Salarino, *masqued*

Gratiano. This is the penthouse under which Lorenzo
Desired us to make stand.

Salarino.   His hour is almost past.

Gratiano. And it is marvel he out-dwells his hour,
For lovers ever run before the clock.

Salarino. O, ten times faster Venus' pigeons fly
To seal love's bonds new-made, than they are wont
To keep obliged faith unforfeited!

Gratiano. That ever holds: who riseth from a feast
With that keen appetite that he sits down?
Where is the horse that doth untread again
His tedious measures with the unbated fire
That he did pace them first? All things that are,
Are with more spirit chased than enjoy'd.
How like a younger or a prodigal

The scarfed bark puts from her native bay,
Hugg'd and embraced by the strumpet wind!
How like the prodigal doth she return
With over-weather'd ribs and ragged sails,
Lean, rent, and beggar'd by the strumpet wind!

Salarino. Here comes Lorenzo: more of this hereafter.
Enter Lorenzo

Lorenzo. Sweet friends, your patience for my long abode
(Not I, but my affairs, have made you wait)
When you shall please to play the thieves for wives,
I'll watch as long for you then. Approach;
Here dwells my father Jew. Ho! Who's within?
Enter Jessica, *above, in boy's clothes*

Jessica. Who are you? Tell me for more certainty,
Albeit I'll swear that I do know your tongue.

Lorenzo. Lorenzo, and thy love.

Jessica. Lorenzo certain, and my love indeed,
For who love I so much? And now who knows
But you, Lorenzo, whether I am yours?

Lorenzo. Heaven and thy thoughts are witness that thou art.

Jessica. Here, catch this casket; it is worth the pains.
I am glad 'tis night, you do not look on me.
For I am much ashamed of my exchange:
But love is blind, and lovers cannot see
The pretty follies that themselves commit,
For if they could, Cupid himself would blush
To see me thus transformed to a boy.

Lorenzo. Descend, for you must be my torch-bearer.

Jessica. What, must I hold a candle to my shames?
They in themselves, good sooth, are too too light.

Why, 'tis an office of discovery, love,
And I should be obscured.

Lorenzo.   So are you, sweet,
Even in the lovely garnish of a boy.
But come at once,
For the close night doth play the runaway,
And we are stay'd for at Bassanio's feast.

Jessica. I will make fast the doors and gild myself
With some mo ducats, and be with you straight.

Exit above.

Gratiano. Now, by my hood, a gentle, and no Jew.

Lorenzo. Beshrew me but I love her heartily,
For she is wise, if I can judge of her,
And fair she is, if that mine eyes be true,
And true she is, as she hath proved herself;
And therefore, like herself, wise, fair, and true,
Shall she be placed in my constant soul.

Enter Jessica, *below*

What, art thou come? On gentlemen, away!
Our masquing mates by this time for us stay.

Exit with Jessica *and* Salarino.

Enter Antonio

Antonio. Who's there?

Gratiano. Signior Antonio!

Antonio. Fie, fie, Gratiano! Where are all the rest?
'Tis nine o'clock, our friends all stay for you.
No masque to-night: the wind is come about;
Bassanio presently will go aboard:
I have sent twenty out to seek for you.

Gratiano. I am glad on't: I desire no more delight
   Than to be under sail and gone tonight.

Exeunt.

scene 7. [*Belmont; A room in* Portia's *house*]

Flourish of cornets. Enter Portia *with the*
Prince of Morocco *and their trains*

Portia. Go draw aside the curtains, and discover
   The several caskets to this noble prince.
   Now make your choice.

Prince of Morocco. The first of gold, who this inscription bears,
   'Who chooseth me shall gain what many men desire';
   The second silver, which this promise carries,
   'Who chooseth me shall get as much as he deserves';
   This third, dull lead, with warning all as blunt,
   'Who chooseth me must give and hazard all he hath.'
   How shall I know if I do choose the right?

Portia. The one of them contains my picture, prince:
   If you choose that, then I am yours withal.

Prince of Morocco. Some god direct my judgement! Let me see,
   I will survey the inscriptions back again.
   What says this leaden casket?
   'Who chooseth me must give and hazard all he hath.'
   Must give,—for what? For lead? Hazard for lead?
   This casket threatens. Men that hazard all
   Do it in hope of fair advantages:
   A golden mind stoops not to shows of dross;
   I'll then nor give nor hazard aught for lead.
   What says the silver with her virgin hue?

'Who chooseth me shall get as much as he deserves.'
As much as he deserves! Pause there, Morocco,
And weigh thy value with an even hand:
If thou be'st rated by thy estimation,
Thou dost deserve enough, and yet enough
May not extend so far as to the lady:
And yet to be afeard of my deserving
Were but a weak disabling of myself.
As much as I deserve! Why, that's the lady:
I do in birth deserve her, and in fortunes,
In graces, and in qualities of breeding;
But more than these, in love I do deserve.
What if I stray'd no further, but chose here?
Let's see once more this saying graved in gold:
'Who chooseth me shall gain what many men desire.'
Why, that's the lady; all the world desires her.
From the four corners of the earth they come
To kiss this shrine, this mortal-breathing saint.
The Hyrcanian deserts and the vasty wilds
Of wide Arabia are as throughfares now
For princes to come view fair Portia:
The watery kingdom, whose ambitious head
Spits in the face of heaven, is no bar
To stop the foreign spirits, but they come
As o'er a brook to see fair Portia.
One of these three contains her heavenly picture.
Is't like that lead contains her? 'Twere damnation
To think so base a thought, it were too gross
To rib her cerecloth in the obscure grave.
Or shall I think in silver she's immured,
Being ten times undervalued to tried gold?
O sinful thought! Never so rich a gem
Was set in worse than gold. They have in England

A coin that bears the figure of an angel
Stamped in gold, but that's insculp'd upon;
But here an angel in a golden bed
Lies all within. Deliver me the key:
Here do I choose, and thrive I as I may!

Portia. There, take it, prince, and if my form lie there,
Then I am yours.

He unlocks the golden casket.

Prince of Morocco.   O hell! What have we here?
A carrion Death, within whose empty eye
There is a written scroll! I'll read the writing.

Reads.

> All that glisters is not gold;
> Often have you heard that told:
> Many a man his life hath sold
> But my outside to behold!
> Gilded tombs do worms infold,
> Had you been as wise as bold,
> Young in limbs, in judgement old,
> Your answer had not been inscroll'd:
> Fare you well; your suit is cold.

Cold indeed, and labour lost:
Then, farewell heat, and welcome frost!
Portia, adieu. I have too grieved a heart
To take a tedious leave: thus losers part.

Exit with his train. Flourish of cornets.

Portia. A gentle riddance. Draw the curtains, go.
Let all of his complexion choose me so.

Exeunt.

scene 8. [*Venice; A street*]

Enter Salarino *and* Salanio

Salarino. Why man, I saw Bassanio under sail:
 With him is Gratiano gone along,
 And in their ship I am sure Lorenzo is not.

Salanio. The villain Jew with outcries raised the Duke,
 Who went with him to search Bassanio's ship.

Salarino. He came too late, the ship was under sail,
 But there the Duke was given to understand
 That in a gondola were seen together
 Lorenzo and his amorous Jessica.
 Besides, Antonio certified the Duke
 They were not with Bassanio in his ship.

Salanio. I never heard a passion so confused,
 So strange, outrageous, and so variable,
 As the dog Jew did utter in the streets:
 'My daughter! O my ducats! O my daughter!
 Fled with a Christian! O my Christian ducats!
 Justice, the law, my ducats, and my daughter!
 A sealed bag, two sealed bags of ducats,
 Of double ducats, stolen from me by my daughter!
 And jewels, two stones, two rich and precious stones,
 Stolen by my daughter! Justice! Find the girl!
 She hath the stones upon her, and the ducats!'

Salarino. Why, all the boys in Venice follow him,
 Crying his stones, his daughter, and his ducats.

Salanio. Let good Antonio look he keep his day,
 Or he shall pay for this.

Salarino.   Marry, well remember'd.
   I reason'd with a Frenchman yesterday,
   Who told me, in the narrow seas that part
   The French and English, there miscarried
   A vessel of our country richly fraught:
   I thought upon Antonio when he told me,
   And wish'd in silence that it were not his.

Salanio. You were best to tell Antonio what you hear,
   Yet do not suddenly, for it may grieve him.

Salarino. A kinder gentleman treads not the earth.
   I saw Bassanio and Antonio part:
   Bassanio told him he would make some speed
   Of his return: he answer'd, 'Do not so,
   Slubber not business for my sake, Bassanio,
   But stay the very riping of the time,
   And for the Jew's bond which he hath of me,
   Let it not enter in your mind of love:
   Be merry, and employ your chiefest thoughts
   To courtship, and such fair ostents of love
   As shall conveniently become you there.'
   And even there, his eye being big with tears,
   Turning his face, he put his hand behind him,
   And with affection wondrous sensible
   He wrung Bassanio's hand, and so they parted.

Salanio. I think he only loves the world for him.
   I pray thee, let us go and find him out,
   And quicken his embraced heaviness
   With some delight or other.

Salarino.   Do we so.

                                          Exeunt.

scene 9. [*Belmont; A room in* Portia's *house*]

Enter Nerissa *and a* Servitor

Nerissa. Quick, quick, I pray thee, draw the curtain straight:
   The Prince of Arragon hath ta'en his oath,
   And comes to his election presently.
            Flourish of cornets. Enter the Prince of Arragon,
                     Portia, *and their trains*

Portia. Behold, there stand the caskets, noble prince:
   If you choose that wherein I am contain'd,
   Straight shall our nuptial rites be solemnized.
   But if you fail, without more speech my lord,
   You must be gone from hence immediately.

Prince of Arragon. I am enjoin'd by oath to observe three things:
   First, never to unfold to any one
   Which casket 'twas I chose; next, if I fail
   Of the right casket, never in my life
   To woo a maid in way of marriage:
   Lastly,
   If I do fail in fortune of my choice,
   Immediately to leave you and be gone.

Portia. To these injunctions every one doth swear
   That comes to hazard for my worthless self.

Prince of Arragon. And so have I address'd me. Fortune now
   To my heart's hope! Gold, silver, and base lead.
   'Who chooseth me must give and hazard all he hath.'
   You shall look fairer ere I give or hazard.
   What says the golden chest? Ha! let me see:
   'Who chooseth me shall gain what many men desire.'
   What many men desire! That 'many' may be meant

By the fool multitude, that choose by show,
Not learning more than the fond eye doth teach,
Which pries not to the interior, but, like the martlet
Builds in the weather on the outward wall,
Even in the force and road of casualty.
I will not choose what many men desire,
Because I will not jump with common spirits,
And rank me with the barbarous multitudes.
Why, then to thee, thou silver treasure-house,
Tell me once more what title thou dost bear:
'Who chooseth me shall get as much as he deserves,'
And well said too; for who shall go about
To cozen fortune, and be honourable
Without the stamp of merit? Let none presume
To wear an undeserved dignity.
O, that estates, degrees, and offices
Were not derived corruptly, and that clear honour
Were purchased by the merit of the wearer!
How many then should cover that stand bare!
How many be commanded that command!
How much low peasantry would then be glean'd
From the true seed of honour! And how much honour
Pick'd from the chaff and ruin of the times,
To be new-varnish'd! Well, but to my choice:
'Who chooseth me shall get as much as he deserves.'
I will assume desert. Give me a key for this,
And instantly unlock my fortunes here.

He opens the silver casket.

Portia. [*Aside*] Too long a pause for that which you find there.

Prince of Arragon. What's here? The portrait of a blinking idiot
Presenting me a schedule! I will read it.
How much unlike art thou to Portia!

How much unlike my hopes and my deservings!
'Who chooseth me shall have as much as he deserves.'
Did I deserve no more than a fool's head?
Is that my prize? Are my deserts no better?

Portia. To offend and judge are distinct offices,
And of opposed natures.

Prince of Arragon.　　　　　What is here?

[*Reads*]　　The fire seven times tried this:
　　　　　Seven times tried that judgement is,
　　　　　That did never choose amiss.
　　　　　Some there be that shadows kiss,
　　　　　Such have but a shadow's bliss:
　　　　　There be fools alive, I wis,
　　　　　Silver'd o'er; and so was this.
　　　　　Take what wife you will to bed,
　　　　　I will ever be your head:
　　　　　So be gone, you are sped.

Still more fool I shall appear
By the time I linger here:
With one fool's head I came to woo,
But I go away with two.
Sweet, adieu. I'll keep my oath,
Patiently to bear my wroth.

Exeunt Arragon *and train.*

Portia. Thus hath the candle singed the moth.
O, these deliberate fools! When they do choose,
They have the wisdom by their wit to lose.

Nerissa. The ancient saying is no heresy,
Hanging and wiving goes by destiny.

Portia. Come draw the curtain Nerissa.

Enter a Servant

Servant. Where is my lady?

Portia.   Here: what would my lord?

Servant. Madam, there is alighted at your gate
　A young Venetian, one that comes before
　To signify th' approaching of his lord,
　From whom he bringeth sensible regreets,
　To wit, besides commends and courteous breath,
　Gifts of rich value. Yet I have not seen
　So likely an ambassador of love:
　A day in April never came so sweet
　To show how costly summer was at hand,
　As this fore-spurrer comes before his lord.

Portia. No more, I pray thee, I am half afeard
　Thou wilt say anon he is some kin to thee,
　Thou spend'st such high-day wit in praising him.
　Come, come Nerissa, for I long to see
　Quick Cupid's post that comes so mannerly.

Nerissa. Bassanio, lord Love, if thy will it be!

Exeunt.

act 3

scene 1. [*Venice; A street*]

Enter Salanio *and* Salarino

Salanio. Now what news on the Rialto?

Salarino. Why, yet it lives there unchecked, that Antonio hath a
ship of rich lading wracked on the narrow seas; the
Goodwins, I think they call the place, a very dangerous flat
and fatal, where the carcases of many a tall ship lie buried, as
they say, if my gossip Report be an honest woman of her
word.

Salanio. I would she were as lying a gossip in that as ever
knapped ginger, or made her neighbours believe she wept for
the death of a third husband. But it is true, without any slips
of prolixity, or crossing the plain highway of talk, that the
good Antonio, the honest Antonio—O that I had a title good
enough to keep his name company!—

Salarino. Come, the full stop.

Salanio. Ha! what sayest thou? Why, the end is, he hath lost a ship.

Salarino. I would it might prove the end of his losses.

Salanio. Let me say 'amen' betimes, lest the devil cross my prayer, for here he comes in the likeness of a Jew.

Enter Shylock

How now, Shylock! What news among the merchants?

Shylock. You knew, none so well, none so well as you, of my daughter's flight.

Salarino. That's certain: I, for my part, knew the tailor that made the wings she flew withal.

Salanio. And Shylock, for his own part, knew the bird was fledged, and then it is the complexion of them all to leave the dam.

Shylock. She is damned for it.

Salarino. That's certain, if the devil may be her judge.

Shylock. My own flesh and blood to rebel!

Salanio. Out upon it, old carrion! Rebels it at these years?

Shylock. I say, my daughter is my flesh and blood.

Salarino. There is more difference between thy flesh and hers than between jet and ivory, more between your bloods than there is between red wine and rhenish. But tell us, do you hear whether Antonio have had any loss at sea or no?

Shylock. There I have another bad match: a bankrupt, a prodigal, who dare scarce show his head on the Rialto, a beggar, that was used to come so smug upon the mart. Let him look to his bond: he was wont to call me usurer; let him look to his bond: he was wont to lend money for a Christian courtesy; let him look to his bond.

Salarino. Why, I am sure if he forfeit, thou wilt not take his flesh: what's that good for?

Shylock. To bait fish withal: if it will feed nothing else, it will feed my revenge. He hath disgraced me, and hindered me half a million, laughed at my losses, mocked at my gains, scorned my nation, thwarted my bargains, cooled my friends, heated mine enemies—and what's his reason? I am a Jew. Hath not a Jew eyes? hath not a Jew hands, organs, dimensions, senses, affections, passions? Fed with the same food, hurt with the same weapons, subject to the same diseases, healed by the same means, warmed and cooled by the same winter and summer as a Christian is? If you prick us, do we not bleed? If you tickle us, do we not laugh? If you poison us, do we not die? And if you wrong us, shall we not revenge? If we are like you in the rest, we will resemble you in that. If a Jew wrong a Christian, what is his humility? Revenge. If a Christian wrong a Jew, what should his sufferance be by Christian example? Why, revenge. The villany you teach me, I will execute; and it shall go hard but I will better the instruction.

Enter a Servant

Servant. Gentlemen, my master Antonio is at his house, and desires to speak with you both.

Salarino. We have been up and down to seek him.

Enter Tubal

Salanio. Here comes another of the tribe: a third cannot be matched, unless the devil himself turn Jew.

Exeunt Salanio, Salarino *and* Servant.

Shylock. How now, Tubal! What news from Genoa? Hast thou found my daughter?

Tubal. I often came where I did hear of her, but cannot find her.

Shylock. Why, there, there, there, there! A diamond gone, cost me two thousand ducats in Frankfort! The curse never fell upon our nation till now, I never felt it till now: two thousand ducats in that, and other precious, precious jewels. I would my daughter were dead at my foot, and the jewels in her ear! Would she were hearsed at my foot, and the ducats in her coffin! No news of them? Why, so:—and I know not what's spent in the search: why, thou loss upon loss! The thief gone with so much, and so much to find the thief; and no satisfaction, no revenge, nor no ill luck stirring but what lights on my shoulders, no sighs but of my breathing, no tears but of my shedding.

Tubal. Yes, other men have ill luck too: Antonio, as I heard in Genoa—

Shylock. What, what, what? Ill luck, ill luck?

Tubal. Hath an argosy cast away, coming from Tripolis.

Shylock. I thank God, I thank God! Is't true, is't true?

Tubal. I spoke with some of the sailors that escaped the wrack.

Shylock. I thank thee, good Tubal: good news, good news! Ha, ha! Heard in Genoa?

Tubal. Your daughter spent in Genoa, as I heard, in one night fourscore ducats.

Shylock. Thou stick'st a dagger in me: I shall never see my gold again: fourscore ducats at a sitting! Fourscore ducats!

Tubal. There came divers of Antonio's creditors in my company to Venice, that swear he cannot choose but break.

Shylock. I am very glad of it: I'll plague him, I'll torture him. I am glad of it.

Tubal. One of them showed me a ring that he had of your daughter for a monkey.

Shylock. Out upon her! Thou torturest me, Tubal: it was my turquoise, I had it of Leah when I was a bachelor: I would not have given it for a wilderness of monkeys.

Tubal. But Antonio is certainly undone.

Shylock. Nay, that's true, that's very true. Go Tubal, fee me an
  officer, bespeak him a fortnight before. I will have the heart
  of him if he forfeit, for were he out of Venice, I can make
  what merchandise I will. Go Tubal, and meet me at our
  synagogue; go, good Tubal, at our synagogue, Tubal.

Exeunt.

scene 2. [*Belmont; A room in* Portia's *house*]

Enter Bassanio, Portia, Gratiano, Nerissa, *and* Attendants

Portia. I pray you tarry, pause a day or two
  Before you hazard, for in choosing wrong
  I lose your company: therefore forbear awhile.
  There's something tells me, but it is not love,
  I would not lose you, and you know yourself,
  Hate counsels not in such a quality.
  But lest you should not understand me well—
  And yet a maiden hath no tongue but thought—
  I would detain you here some month or two
  Before you venture for me. I could teach you
  How to choose right, but I am then forsworn,
  So will I never be: so may you miss me.
  But if you do, you'll make me wish a sin,
  That I had been forsworn. Beshrew your eyes,
  They have o'er-look'd me and divided me;
  One half of me is yours, the other half yours,
  Mine own, I would say, but if mine then yours,
  And so all yours! O, these naughty times
  Put bars between the owners and their rights!
  And so though yours, not yours. Prove it so,
  Let fortune go to hell for it, not I.
  I speak too long; but 'tis to peize the time,

To eke it and to draw it out in length,
To stay you from election.

Bassanio.   Let me choose,
For as I am, I live upon the rack.

Portia. Upon the rack, Bassanio! Then confess
What treason there is mingled with your love.

Bassanio. None but that ugly treason of mistrust,
Which makes me fear the enjoying of my love:
There may as well be amity and life
'Tween snow and fire, as treason and my love.

Portia. Ay, but I fear you speak upon the rack
Where men enforced do speak any thing.

Bassanio. Promise me life, and I'll confess the truth.

Portia. Well then, confess and live.

Bassanio.   'Confess' and 'love'
Had been the very sum of my confession:
O happy torment, when my torturer
Doth teach me answers for deliverance!
But let me to my fortune and the caskets.

Portia. Away then! I am lock'd in one of them:
If you do love me, you will find me out.
Nerissa and the rest, stand all aloof.
Let music sound while he doth make his choice,
Then if he lose he makes a swan-like end,
Fading in music. That the comparison
May stand more proper, my eye shall be the stream,
And watery death-bed for him. He may win,
And what is music then? Then music is
Even as the flourish when true subjects bow
To a new-crowned monarch: such it is
As are those dulcet sounds in break of day

That creep into the dreaming bridegroom's ear,
And summon him to marriage. Now he goes
With no less presence, but with much more love
Than young Alcides, when he did redeem
The virgin tribute paid by howling Troy
To the sea-monster: I stand for sacrifice,
The rest aloof are the Dardanian wives
With bleared visages come forth to view
The issue of the exploit. Go, Hercules!
Live thou, I live: with much much more dismay
I view the fight than thou that mak'st the fray.

Music, whilst Bassanio *comments on the caskets to himself.*

Song

> Tell me where is fancy bred,
> Or in the heart or in the head?
> How begot, how nourished?
> > Reply, reply.
> It is engender'd in the eyes,
> With gazing fed, and fancy dies
> In the cradle where it lies.
> > Let us all ring fancy's knell.
> > I'll begin it—Ding, dong, bell.

All.   Ding, dong, bell.

Bassanio. So may the outward shows he least themselves:
    The world is still deceived with ornament.
    In law, what plea so tainted and corrupt,
    But, being season'd with a gracious voice,
    Obscures the show of evil? In religion,
    What damned error, but some sober brow
    Will bless it, and approve it with a text,
    Hiding the grossness with fair ornament?
    There is no vice so simple, but assumes
    Some mark of virtue on his outward parts:

How many cowards, whose hearts are all as false
As stairs of sand, wear yet upon their chins
The beards of Hercules and frowning Mars,
Who inward search'd, have livers white as milk?
And these assume but valour's excrement
To render them redoubted! Look on beauty,
And you shall see 'tis purchased by the weight,
Which therein works a miracle in nature,
Making them lightest that wear most of it:
So are those crisped snaky golden locks
Which make such wanton gambols with the wind
Upon supposed fairness, often known
To be the dowry of a second head,
The skull that bred them in the sepulchre.
Thus ornament is but the guiled shore
To a most dangerous sea, the beauteous scarf
Veiling an Indian beauty; in a word,
The seeming truth which cunning times put on
To entrap the wisest. Therefore thou gaudy gold,
Hard food for Midas, I will none of thee,
Nor none of thee, thou pale and common drudge
'Tween man and man: but thou, thou meagre lead,
Which rather threatenest than dost promise aught,
Thy paleness moves me more than eloquence,
And here choose I: joy be the consequence!

Portia. [*Aside*] How all the other passions fleet to air,
As doubtful thoughts, and rash-embraced despair,
And shuddering fear, and green-eyed jealousy!
O love, be moderate; allay thy ecstasy,
In measure rain thy joy, scant this excess!
I feel too much thy blessing: make it less,
For fear I surfeit!

Bassanio.   What find I here?

Opening the leaden casket.

Fair Portia's counterfeit! What demi–god
Hath come so near creation? Move these eyes?
Or whether, riding on the balls of mine,
Seem they in motion? Here are sever'd lips
Parted with sugar breath: so sweet a bar
Should sunder such sweet friends. Here in her hairs
The painter plays the spider, and hath woven
A golden mesh t' entrap the hearts of men
Faster than gnats in cobwebs: but her eyes
How could he see to do them? Having made one,
Methinks it should have power to steal both his
And leave itself unfurnish'd. Yet look, how far
The substance of my praise doth wrong this shadow
In underprizing it, so far this shadow
Doth limp behind the substance. Here's the scroll,
The continent and summary of my fortune.

[*Reads*]   You that choose not by the view
                  Chance as fair, and choose as true!
                  Since this fortune falls to you,
                  Be content and seek no new.
                  If you be well pleased with this,
                  And hold your fortune for your bliss,
                  Turn you where your lady is,
                  And claim her with a loving kiss.

A gentle scroll. Fair lady, by your leave,
I come by note to give and to receive.
Like one of two contending in a prize
That thinks he hath done well in people's eyes,
Hearing applause and universal shout,
Giddy in spirit, still gazing in a doubt
Whether those peals of praise be his or no;

So, thrice-fair lady, stand I even so;
As doubtful whether what I see be true,
Until confirm'd, sign'd, ratified by you.

Portia. You see me, Lord Bassanio, where I stand,
Such as I am: though for myself alone
I would not be ambitious in my wish
To wish myself much better, yet for you
I would be trebled twenty times myself,
A thousand times more fair, ten thousand times
More rich,
That only to stand high in your account,
I might in virtues, beauties, livings, friends
Exceed account; but the full sum of me
Is sum of something, which to term in gross,
Is an unlesson'd girl, unschool'd, unpractised.
Happy in this, she is not yet so old
But she may learn; happier than this,
She is not bred so dull but she can learn;
Happiest of all is that her gentle spirit
Commits itself to yours to be directed,
As from her lord, her governor, her king.
Myself and what is mine to you and yours
Is now converted: but now I was the lord
Of this fair mansion, master of my servants,
Queen o'er myself; and even now, but now,
This house, these servants, and this same myself
Are yours, my lord: I give them with this ring,
Which when you part from, lose, or give away,
Let it presage the ruin of your love,
And be my vantage to exclaim on you.

Bassanio. Madam, you have bereft me of all words,
Only my blood speaks to you in my veins,

And there is such confusion in my powers,
As after some oration fairly spoke
By a beloved prince, there doth appear
Among the buzzing pleased multitude,
Where every something being blent together,
Turns to a wild of nothing, save of joy
Express'd and not express'd. But when this ring.
Parts from this finger, then parts life from hence:
O, then be bold to say Bassanio's dead!

Nerissa. My lord and lady, it is now our time
    That have stood by and seen our wishes prosper,
    To cry good joy: good joy, my lord and lady!

Gratiano. My Lord Bassanio and my gentle lady,
    I wish you all the joy that you can wish,
    For I am sure you can wish none from me:
    And when your honours mean to solemnize
    The bargain of your faith, I do beseech you
    Even at that time I may be married too.

Bassanio. With all my heart, so thou canst get a wife.

Gratiano. I thank your lordship, you have got me one.
    My eyes, my lord, can look as swift as yours:
    You saw the mistress, I beheld the maid;
    You loved, I loved, for intermission.
    No more pertains to me, my lord, than you.
    Your fortune stood upon the casket there,
    And so did mine too, as the matter falls;
    For wooing here until I sweat again,
    And swearing till my very roof was dry
    With oaths of love, at last, if promise last,
    I got a promise of this fair one here
    To have her love, provided that your fortune
    Achieved her mistress.

Portia.   Is this true, Nerissa?

Nerissa. Madam it is, so you stand pleased withal.

Bassanio. And do you, Gratiano, mean good faith?

Gratiano. Yes, faith my lord.

Bassanio. Our feast shall be much honoured in your marriage.

Gratiano. We'll play with them the first boy for a thousand
     ducats.

Nerissa. What, and stake down?

Gratiano. No, we shall ne'er win at that sport, and stake down.
     But who comes here? Lorenzo and his infidel!
     What, and my old Venetian friend Salerio?
          Enter Lorenzo, Jessica, *and* Salerio, *a Messenger from Venice*

Bassanio. Lorenzo and Salerio, welcome hither,
     If that the youth of my new interest here
     Have power to bid you welcome. By your leave
     I bid my very friends and countrymen,
     Sweet Portia, welcome.

Portia.   So do I, my lord:
     They are entirely welcome.

Lorenzo. I thank your honour. For my part, my lord,
     My purpose was not to have seen you here,
     But meeting with Salerio by the way,
     He did entreat me, past all saying nay,
     To come with him along.

Salerio.   I did, my lord,
     And I have reason for it. Signior Antonio
     Commends him to you.

                              Gives Bassanio *a letter.*

Bassanio.   Ere I ope his letter,
     I pray you, tell me how my good friend doth.

Salerio. Not sick, my lord, unless it be in mind;
    Nor well, unless in mind: his letter there
    Will show you his estate.

Gratiano. Nerissa, cheer yon stranger, bid her welcome.
    Your hand, Salerio: what's the news from Venice?
    How doth that royal merchant good Antonio?
    I know he will be glad of our success;
    We are the Jasons, we have won the fleece.

Salerio. I would you had won the fleece that he hath lost.

Portia. There are some shrewd contents in yond same paper
    That steals the colour from Bassanio's cheek:
    Some dear friend dead, else nothing in the world
    Could turn so much the constitution
    Of any constant man. What, worse and worse!
    With leave, Bassanio, I am half yourself,
    And I must freely have the half of anything
    That this same paper brings you.

Bassanio.   O sweet Portia,
    Here are a few of the unpleasant'st words
    That ever blotted paper! Gentle lady
    When I did first impart my love to you,
    I freely told you, all the wealth I had
    Ran in my veins, I was a gentleman.
    And then I told you true: and yet dear lady,
    Rating myself at nothing, you shall see
    How much I was a braggart. When I told you
    My state was nothing, I should then have told you
    That I was worse than nothing, for indeed
    I have engaged myself to a dear friend,
    Engaged my friend to his mere enemy,
    To feed my means. Here is a letter, lady:
    The paper as the body of my friend,

And every word in it a gaping wound
Issuing life-blood. But is it true, Salerio?
Have all his ventures fail'd? What, not one hit?
From Tripolis, from Mexico and England,
From Lisbon, Barbary, and India?
And not one vessel scape the dreadful touch
Of merchant-marring rocks?

Salerio.   Not one, my lord.
Besides, it should appear, that if he had
The present money to discharge the Jew,
He would not take it. Never did I know
A creature, that did bear the shape of man,
So keen and greedy to confound a man:
He plies the Duke at morning and at night,
And doth impeach the freedom of the state,
If they deny him justice. Twenty merchants,
The Duke himself, and the magnificoes
Of greatest port have all persuaded with him,
But none can drive him from the envious plea
Of forfeiture, of justice, and his bond.

Jessica. When I was with him I have heard him swear
To Tubal and to Chus, his countrymen,
That he would rather have Antonio's flesh
Than twenty times the value of the sum
That he did owe him: and I know my lord,
If law, authority, and power deny not,
It will go hard with poor Antonio.

Portia. Is it your dear friend that is thus in trouble?

Bassanio. The dearest friend to me, the kindest man,
The best-condition'd and unwearied spirit
In doing courtesies, and one in whom

The ancient Roman honour more appears
Than any that draws breath in Italy.

Portia. What sum owes he the Jew?

Bassanio. For me three thousand ducats.

Portia.   What, no more?
Pay him six thousand, and deface the bond.
Double six thousand, and then treble that,
Before a friend of this description
Shall lose a hair through Bassanio's fault.
First go with me to church and call me wife,
And then away to Venice to your friend,
For never shall you lie by Portia's side
With an unquiet soul. You shall have gold
To pay the petty debt twenty times over:
When it is paid, bring your true friend along.
My maid Nerissa and myself meantime
Will live as maids and widows. Come, away!
For you shall hence upon your wedding day:
Bid your friends welcome, show a merry cheer—
Since you are dear bought, I will love you dear.
But let me hear the letter of your friend.

Bassanio. [*Reads*] Sweet Bassanio, my ships have all miscarried, my creditors
grow cruel, my estate is very low, my bond to the Jew is forfeit, and since in
paying it, it is impossible I should live, all debts are cleared between you and
I, if I might but see you at my death. Notwithstanding, use your pleasure:
if your love do not persuade you to come, let not my letter.

Portia. O love, dispatch all business, and be gone!

Bassanio. Since I have your good leave to go away,
I will make haste, but till I come again,
No bed shall e'er be guilty of my stay,
No rest be interposer 'twixt us twain.

                                                        Exeunt.

scene 3. [*Venice; A street*]

Enter Shylock, Salarino, Antonio, *and* Gaoler

Shylock. Gaoler, look to him—tell not me of mercy—
This is the fool that lent out money gratis:
Gaoler, look to him.

Antonio.   Hear me yet, good Shylock.

Shylock. I'll have my bond, speak not against my bond:
I have sworn an oath that I will have my bond.
Thou call'dst me dog before thou hadst a cause,
But, since I am a dog, beware my fangs:
The Duke shall grant me justice. I do wonder,
Thou naughty gaoler, that thou art so fond
To come abroad with him at his request.

Antonio. I pray thee, hear me speak.

Shylock. I'll have my bond. I will not hear thee speak:
I'll have my bond, and therefore speak no more.
I'll not be made a soft and dull-eyed fool,
To shake the head, relent, and sigh, and yield
To Christian intercessors. Follow not:
I'll have no speaking. I will have my bond.

Exit.

Salarino. It is the most impenetrable cur
That ever kept with men.

Antonio.   Let him alone,
I'll follow him no more with bootless prayers.
He seeks my life, his reason well I know:
I oft deliver'd from his forfeitures
Many that have at times made moan to me;
Therefore he hates me.

Salarino.   I am sure the Duke
   Will never grant this forfeiture to hold.

Antonio. The Duke cannot deny the course of law:
   For the commodity that strangers have
   With us in Venice, if it be denied,
   Will much impeach the justice of his state,
   Since that the trade and profit of the city
   Consisteth of all nations. Therefore go:
   These griefs and losses have so bated me
   That I shall hardly spare a pound of flesh
   Tomorrow to my bloody creditor.
   Well, gaoler, on. Pray God Bassanio come
   To see me pay his debt, and then I care not.

                                        Exeunt.

scene 4.   [*Belmont; A room in* Portia's *house*]

Enter Portia, Nerissa, Lorenzo, Jessica, *and* Balthasar

Lorenzo. Madam, although I speak it in your presence,
   You have a noble and a true conceit
   Of god-like amity, which appears most strongly
   In bearing thus the absence of your lord.
   But if you knew to whom you show this honour,
   How true a gentleman you send relief,
   How dear a lover of my lord your husband,
   I know you would be prouder of the work
   Than customary bounty can enforce you.

Portia. I never did repent for doing good,
   Nor shall not now: for in companions
   That do converse and waste the time together,
   Whose souls do bear an equal yoke of love,

There must be needs a like proportion
Of lineaments, of manners, and of spirit;
Which makes me think that this Antonio,
Being the bosom lover of my lord,
Must needs be like my lord. If it be so,
How little is the cost I have bestow'd
In purchasing the semblance of my soul
From out the state of hellish cruelty!
This comes too near the praising of myself,
Therefore no more of it: hear other things.
Lorenzo, I commit into your hands
The husbandry and manage of my house
Until my lord's return: for mine own part,
I have toward heaven breathed a secret vow
To live in prayer and contemplation,
Only attended by Nerissa here,
Until her husband and my lord's return.
There is a monastery two miles off,
And there will we abide. I do desire you
Not to deny this imposition,
The which my love and some necessity
Now lays upon you.

Lorenzo.　　　　　Madam, with all my heart,
I shall obey you in all fair commands.

Portia. My people do already know my mind,
And will acknowledge you and Jessica
In place of Lord Bassanio and myself.
And so farewell, till we shall meet again.

Lorenzo. Fair thoughts and happy hours attend on you!

Jessica. I wish your ladyship all heart's content.

Portia. I thank you for your wish, and am well pleased
    To wish it back on you: fare you well, Jessica.

                        Exeunt Jessica *and* Lorenzo.
    Now, Balthasar,
    As I have ever found thee honest-true,
    So let me find thee still. Take this same letter,
    And use thou all the endeavour of a man
    In speed to Padua: see thou render this
    Into my cousin's hand, Doctor Bellario,
    And look what notes and garments he doth give thee.
    Bring them, I pray thee, with imagined speed
    Unto the traject, to the common ferry
    Which trades to Venice. Waste no time in words,
    But get thee gone: I shall be there before thee.

Balthasar. Madam, I go with all convenient speed.

                               Exit.

Portia. Come on Nerissa, I have work in hand
    That you yet know not of; we'll see our husbands
    Before they think of us.

Nerissa.   Shall they see us?

Portia. They shall, Nerissa, but in such a habit
    That they shall think we are accomplished
    With that we lack. I'll hold thee any wager,
    When we are both accoutred like young men,
    I'll prove the prettier fellow of the two,
    And wear my dagger with the braver grace,
    And speak between the change of man and boy
    With a reed voice, and turn two mincing steps
    Into a manly stride, and speak of frays
    Like a fine bragging youth; and tell quaint lies
    How honourable ladies sought my love,

Which I denying, they fell sick and died;
I could not do withal: then I'll repent,
And wish for all that, that I had not kill'd them.
And twenty of these puny lies I'll tell,
That men shall swear I have discontinued school
Above a twelvemonth. I have within my mind
A thousand raw tricks of these bragging Jacks,
Which I will practise.

Nerissa.   Why, shall we turn to men?

Portia. Fie, what a question's that,
If thou wert near a lewd interpreter!
But come, I'll tell thee all my whole device
When I am in my coach, which stays for us
At the park gate; and therefore haste away,
For we must measure twenty miles today.

                                        Exeunt.

scene 5.   [*The same; A garden*]

Enter Launcelot *and* Jessica

Launcelot. Yes truly, for look you, the sins of the father are to be laid upon the children: therefore, I promise ye, I fear you. I was always plain with you, and so now I speak my agitation of the matter: therefore be of good cheer, for truly I think you are damned. There is but one hope in it that can do you any good, and that is but a kind of bastard hope neither.

Jessica. And what hope is that, I pray thee?

Launcelot. Marry, you may partly hope that your father got you not, that you are not the Jew's daughter.

Jessica. That were a kind of bastard hope indeed, so the sins of my mother should be visited upon me.

Launcelot. Truly then I fear you are damned both by father and mother: thus when I shun Scylla, your father, I fall into Charybdis, your mother. Well, you are gone both ways.

Jessica. I shall be saved by my husband; he hath made me a Christian.

Launcelot. Truly, the more to blame he: we were Christians enow before, e'en as many as could well live, one by another. This making of Christians will raise the price of hogs: if we grow all to be pork-eaters, we shall not shortly have a rasher on the coals for money.

Enter Lorenzo

Jessica. I'll tell my husband, Launcelot, what you say: here he comes.

Lorenzo. I shall grow jealous of you shortly, Launcelot, if you thus get my wife into corners.

Jessica. Nay, you need not fear us, Lorenzo: Launcelot and I are out. He tells me flatly there is no mercy for me in heaven, because I am a Jew's daughter: and he says you are no good member of the commonwealth, for in converting Jews to Christians, you raise the price of pork.

Lorenzo. I shall answer that better to the commonwealth than you can the getting up of the negro's belly: the Moor is with child by you, Launcelot.

Launcelot. It is much that the Moor should be more than reason: but if she be less than an honest woman, she is indeed more than I took her for.

Lorenzo. How every fool can play upon the word! I think the best grace of wit will shortly turn into silence, and discourse grow commendable in none only but parrots. Go in sirrah, bid them prepare for dinner.

Launcelot. That is done sir, they have all stomachs.

Lorenzo. Goodly Lord, what a wit-snapper are you! Then bid them prepare dinner.

Launcelot. That is done too sir, only 'cover' is the word.

Lorenzo. Will you cover then, sir?

Launcelot. Not so sir, neither; I know my duty.

Lorenzo. Yet more quarrelling with occasion! Wilt thou show the whole wealth of thy wit in an instant? I pray thee, understand a plain man in his plain meaning: go to thy fellows, bid them cover the table, serve in the meat, and we will come in to dinner.

Launcelot. For the table sir, it shall be served in; for the meat sir, it shall be covered; for your coming in to dinner sir, why, let it be as humours and conceits shall govern.

Exit.

Lorenzo. O dear discretion, how his words are suited!
  The fool hath planted in his memory
  An army of good words, and I do know
  A many fools that stand in better place,
  Garnish'd like him, that for a tricksy word
  Defy the matter. How cheer'st thou, Jessica?
  And now, good sweet, say thy opinion,
  How dost thou like the Lord Bassanio's wife?

Jessica. Past all expressing. It is very meet
  The Lord Bassanio live an upright life
  For having such a blessing in his lady,
  He finds the joys of heaven here on earth,
  And if on earth he do not mean it,
  In reason he should never come to heaven.
  Why, if two gods should play some heavenly match
  And on the wager lay two earthly women,
  And Portia one, there must be something else

Pawn'd with the other, for the poor rude world
Hath not her fellow.

Lorenzo.   Even such a husband
Hast thou of me, as she is for a wife.

Jessica. Nay, but ask my opinion too of that.

Lorenzo. I will anon: first, let us go to dinner.

Jessica. Nay, let me praise you while I have a stomach.

Lorenzo. No, pray thee, let it serve for table-talk,
Then howsoe'er thou speak'st, 'mong other things
I shall digest it.

Jessica. Well, I'll set you forth.

                                    Exeunt.

act 4

scene 1. [*Venice; A court of justice*]

Enter the Duke, *the* Magnificoes, Antonio,
Bassanio, Gratiano, Salerio, *and others*

Duke. What, is Antonio here?

Antonio. Ready, so please your Grace.

Duke. I am sorry for thee: thou art come to answer
A stony adversary, an inhuman wretch
Uncapable of pity, void and empty
From any dram of mercy.

Antonio.   I have heard
Your Grace hath ta'en great pains to qualify
His rigorous course; but since he stands obdurate,
And that no lawful means can carry me
Out of his envy's reach, I do oppose
My patience to his fury, and am arm'd
To suffer with a quietness of spirit,
The very tyranny and rage of his.

Duke. Go one and call the Jew into the court.

Salerio. He is ready at the door: he comes, my lord.

Enter Shylock

Duke. Make room, and let him stand before our face.
　　Shylock, the world thinks, and I think so too,
　　That thou but lead'st this fashion of thy malice
　　To the last hour of act, and then 'tis thought
　　Thou'lt show thy mercy and remorse more strange
　　Than is thy strange apparent cruelty;
　　And where thou now exact'st the penalty,
　　Which is a pound of this poor merchant's flesh,
　　Thou wilt not only loose the forfeiture,
　　But touch'd with human gentleness and love,
　　Forgive a moiety of the principal,
　　Glancing an eye of pity on his losses
　　That have of late so huddled on his back,
　　Enow to press a royal merchant down,
　　And pluck commiseration of his state
　　From brassy bosoms and rough hearts of flint,
　　From stubborn Turks and Tartars never train'd
　　To offices of tender courtesy.
　　We all expect a gentle answer, Jew.

Shylock. I have possess'd your Grace of what I purpose,
　　And by our holy Sabbath have I sworn
　　To have the due and forfeit of my bond:
　　If you deny it, let the danger light
　　Upon your charter and your city's freedom.
　　You'll ask me, why I rather choose to have
　　A weight of carrion-flesh than to receive
　　Three thousand ducats: I'll not answer that,
　　But say it is my humour: is it answer'd?
　　What if my house be troubled with a rat,
　　And I be pleased to give ten thousand ducats

To have it baned? What, are you answer'd yet?
Some men there are love not a gaping pig,
Some, that are mad if they behold a cat,
And others, when the bagpipe sings i' the nose,
Cannot contain their urine: for affection,
Mistress of passion, sways it to the mood
Of what it likes or loathes. Now for your answer:
As there is no firm reason to be render'd
Why he cannot abide a gaping pig,
Why he a harmless necessary cat,
Why he a woollen bag-pipe, but of force
Must yield to such inevitable shame
As to offend, himself being offended.
So can I give no reason, nor I will not,
More than a lodged hate and a certain loathing
I bear Antonio, that I follow thus
A losing suit against him. Are you answer'd?

Bassanio. This is no answer, thou unfeeling man,
   To excuse the current of thy cruelty.

Shylock. I am not bound to please thee with my answer.

Bassanio. Do all men kill the things they do not love?

Shylock. Hates any man the thing he would not kill?

Bassanio. Every offence is not a hate at first.

Shylock. What, wouldst thou have a serpent sting thee twice?

Antonio. I pray you, think you question with the Jew:
   You may as well go stand upon the beach
   And bid the main flood bate his usual height;
   You may as well use question with the wolf,
   Why he hath made the ewe bleat for the lamb;
   You may as well forbid the mountain pines
   To wag their high tops, and to make no noise

When they are fretten with the gusts of heaven;
You may as well do any thing most hard
As seek to soften that—than which what's harder?—
His Jewish heart. Therefore, I do beseech you,
Make no more offers, use no farther means,
But with all brief and plain conveniency
Let me have judgement and the Jew his will.

Bassanio. For thy three thousand ducats here is six.

Shylock. If every ducat in six thousand ducats
Were in six parts, and every part a ducat,
I would not draw them; I would have my bond.

Duke. How shalt thou hope for mercy, rendering none?

Shylock. What judgement shall I dread, doing no wrong?
You have among you many a purchased slave,
Which, like your asses and your dogs and mules,
You use in abject and in slavish parts
Because you bought them: shall I say to you,
Let them be free, marry them to your heirs?
Why sweat they under burthens? Let their beds
Be made as soft as yours, and let their palates
Be season'd with such viands? You will answer
'The slaves are ours': so do I answer you:
The pound of flesh which I demand of him
Is dearly bought; 'tis mine and I will have it.
If you deny me, fie upon your law!
There is no force in the decrees of Venice.
I stand for judgement: answer, shall I have it?

Duke. Upon my power I may dismiss this court,
Unless Bellario, a learned doctor
Whom I have sent for to determine this,
Come here today.

Salerio.   My lord, here stays without
   A messenger with letters from the doctor,
   New come from Padua.

Duke. Bring us the letters; call the messenger.

Bassanio. Good cheer, Antonio! What, man, courage yet!
   The Jew shall have my flesh, blood, bones, and all,
   Ere thou shalt lose for me one drop of blood.

Antonio. I am a tainted wether of the flock,
   Meetest for death: the weakest kind of fruit
   Drops earliest to the ground, and so let me.
   You cannot better be employ'd, Bassanio,
   Than to live still and write mine epitaph.
           Enter Nerissa, *dressed like a lawyer's clerk*

Duke. Came you from Padua, from Bellario?

Nerissa. From both, my lord. Bellario greets your Grace.
                    Presenting a letter.

Bassanio. Why dost thou whet thy knife so earnestly?

Shylock. To cut the forfeiture from that bankrupt there.

Gratiano. Not on thy sole, but on thy soul, harsh Jew,
   Thou makest thy knife keen; but no metal can,
   No, not the hangman's axe, bear half the keenness
   Of thy sharp envy. Can no prayers pierce thee?

Shylock. No, none that thou hast wit enough to make.

Gratiano. O, be thou damn'd, inexecrable dog!
   And for thy life let justice be accused.
   Thou almost makest me waver in my faith,
   To hold opinion with Pythagoras
   That souls of animals infuse themselves
   Into the trunks of men: thy currish spirit

Govern'd a wolf, who hang'd for human slaughter,
Even from the gallows did his fell soul fleet,
And, whilst thou lay'st in thy unhallow'd dam,
Infused itself in thee, for thy desires
Are wolvish, bloody, starved, and ravenous.

Shylock. Till thou canst rail the seal from off my bond,
Thou but offend'st thy lungs to speak so loud:
Repair thy wit, good youth, or it will fall
To cureless ruin. I stand here for law.

Duke. This letter from Bellario doth commend
A young and learned doctor to our court.
Where is he?

Nerissa.　　　　He attendeth here hard by,
To know your answer, whether you'll admit him.

Duke. With all my heart. Some three or four of you
Go give him courteous conduct to this place.
Meantime the court shall hear Bellario's letter.

Clerk. [*Reads*] Your Grace shall understand that at the receipt of your letter
I am very sick: but in the instant that your messenger came, in loving visi-
tation was with me a young doctor of Rome; his name is Balthasar. I acquainted him with the cause in controversy between the Jew and Antonio
the merchant, we turned o'er many books together, he is furnished with
my opinion, which bettered with his own learning—the greatness whereof
I cannot enough commend—comes with him at my importunity, to fill up
your Grace's request in my stead. I beseech you, let his lack of years be no
impediment to let him lack a reverend estimation, for I never knew so
young a body with so old a head. I leave him to your gracious acceptance,
whose trial shall better publish his commendation.

Duke. You hear the learn'd Bellario what he writes,
And here, I take it, is the doctor come.
　　　　　　　Enter Portia, *as* Balthasar
Give me your hand. Come you from old Bellario?

Portia. I did, my lord.

Duke.   You are welcome: take your place.
    Are you acquainted with the difference
    That holds this present question in the court?

Portia. I am informed throughly of the cause.
    Which is the merchant here, and which the Jew?

Duke. Antonio and old Shylock, both stand forth.

Portia. Is your name Shylock?

Shylock.   Shylock is my name.

Portia. Of a strange nature is the suit you follow,
    Yet in such rule that the Venetian law
    Cannot impugn you as you do proceed.
    You stand within his danger, do you not?

Antonio. Ay, so he says.

Portia.   Do you confess the bond?

Antonio. I do.

Portia.   Then must the Jew be merciful.

Shylock. On what compulsion must I? Tell me that.

Portia. The quality of mercy is not strain'd,
    It droppeth as the gentle rain from heaven
    Upon the place beneath: it is twice blest,
    It blesseth him that gives, and him that takes,
    'Tis mightiest in the mightiest, it becomes
    The throned monarch better than his crown.
    His sceptre shows the force of temporal power,
    The attribute to awe and majesty,
    Wherein doth sit the dread and fear of kings;
    But mercy is above this sceptred sway,
    It is enthroned in the hearts of kings,
    It is an attribute to God himself;

And earthly power doth then show likest God's
When mercy seasons justice. Therefore Jew,
Though justice be thy plea, consider this,
That in the course of justice, none of us
Should see salvation: we do pray for mercy,
And that same prayer doth teach us all to render
The deeds of mercy. I have spoke thus much
To mitigate the justice of thy plea,
Which if thou follow, this strict court of Venice
Must needs give sentence 'gainst the merchant there.

Shylock. My deeds upon my head! I crave the law,
The penalty and forfeit of my bond.

Portia. Is he not able to discharge the money?

Bassanio. Yes, here I tender it for him in the court,
Yea, twice the sum: if that will not suffice,
I will be bound to pay it ten times o'er
On forfeit of my hands, my head, my heart.
If this will not suffice, it must appear
That malice bears down truth. And I beseech you,
Wrest once the law to your authority:
To do a great right, do a little wrong,
And curb this cruel devil of his will.

Portia. It must not be, there is no power in Venice
Can alter a decree established:
'Twill be recorded for a precedent,
And many an error by the same example
Will rush into the state: it cannot be.

Shylock. A Daniel come to judgement! Yea, a Daniel!
O wise young judge, how I do honour thee!

Portia. I pray you, let me look upon the bond.

Shylock. Here 'tis, most reverend doctor, here it is.

Portia. Shylock, there's thrice thy money offer'd thee.

Shylock. An oath, an oath, I have an oath in heaven:
     Shall I lay perjury upon my soul?
     No, not for Venice.

Portia.   Why, this bond is forfeit,
     And lawfully by this the Jew may claim
     A pound of flesh, to be by him cut off
     Nearest the merchant's heart. Be merciful:
     Take thrice thy money, bid me tear the bond.

Shylock. When it is paid according to the tenour.
     It doth appear you are a worthy judge,
     You know the law, your exposition
     Hath been most sound: I charge you by the law,
     Whereof you are a well-deserving pillar,
     Proceed to judgement: by my soul I swear
     There is no power in the tongue of man
     To alter me—I stay here on my bond.

Antonio. Most heartily I do beseech the court
     To give the judgement.

Portia.   Why then, thus it is:
     You must prepare your bosom for his knife.

Shylock. O noble judge! O excellent young man!

Portia. For the intent and purpose of the law
     Hath full relation to the penalty,
     Which here appeareth due upon the bond.

Shylock. 'Tis very true: O wise and upright judge!
     How much more elder art thou than thy looks!

Portia. Therefore lay bare your bosom.

Shylock.   Ay, his breast,
     So says the bond:—doth it not, noble judge?—
     'Nearest his heart': those are the very words.

Portia. It is so. Are there balance here to weigh
  The flesh?

Shylock. I have them ready.

Portia. Have by some surgeon, Shylock, on your charge,
  To stop his wounds, lest he do bleed to death.

Shylock. Is it so nominated in the bond?

Portia. It is not so express'd, but what of that?
  'Twere good you do so much for charity.

Shylock. I cannot find it; 'tis not in the bond.

Portia. You, merchant, have you anything to say?

Antonio. But little: I am arm'd and well prepared.
  Give me your hand, Bassanio: fare you well!
  Grieve not that I am fallen to this for you,
  For herein Fortune shows herself more kind
  Than is her custom: it is still her use
  To let the wretched man outlive his wealth,
  To view with hollow eye and wrinkled brow
  An age of poverty, from which lingering penance
  Of such misery doth she cut me off.
  Commend me to your honourable wife,
  Tell her the process of Antonio's end,
  Say how I loved you, speak me fair in death,
  And when the tale is told, bid her be judge
  Whether Bassanio had not once a love.
  Repent but you that you shall lose your friend
  And he repents not that he pays your debt,
  For if the Jew do cut but deep enough,
  I'll pay it presently with all my heart.

Bassanio. Antonio, I am married to a wife
  Which is as dear to me as life itself;
  But life itself, my wife, and all the world,

Are not with me esteem'd above thy life:
I would lose all, ay, sacrifice them all
Here to this devil, to deliver you.

Portia. Your wife would give you little thanks for that,
If she were by to hear you make the offer.

Gratiano. I have a wife whom I protest I love:
I would she were in heaven, so she could
Entreat some power to change this currish Jew.

Nerissa. 'Tis well you offer it behind her back;
The wish would make else an unquiet house.

Shylock. These be the Christian husbands. I have a daughter;
Would any of the stock of Barrabas
Had been her husband rather than a Christian!   *[Aside]*
We trifle time: I pray thee, pursue sentence.

Portia. A pound of that same merchant's flesh is thine:
The court awards it, and the law doth give it.

Shylock. Most rightful judge!

Portia. And you must cut this flesh from off his breast:
The law allows it, and the court awards it.

Shylock. Most learned judge! A sentence! Come, prepare!

Portia. Tarry a little, there is something else.
This bond doth give thee here no jot of blood,
The words expressly are 'a pound of flesh'.
Take then thy bond, take thou thy pound of flesh,
But in the cutting it, if thou dost shed
One drop of Christian blood, thy lands and goods
Are, by the laws of Venice, confiscate
Unto the state of Venice.

Gratiano. O upright judge! Mark, Jew: O learned judge!

Shylock. Is that the law?

Portia. Thyself shalt see the act:
  For, as thou urgest justice, be assured
  Thou shalt have justice, more than thou desirest.

Gratiano. O learned judge! Mark, Jew, a learned judge!

Shylock. I take this offer, then; pay the bond thrice,
  And let the Christian go.

Bassanio. Here is the money.

Portia. Soft!
  The Jew shall have all justice; soft! No haste:
  He shall have nothing but the penalty.

Gratiano. O Jew! An upright judge, a learned judge!

Portia. Therefore prepare thee to cut off the flesh.
  Shed thou no blood, nor cut thou less nor more
  But just a pound of flesh: if thou cut'st more
  Or less than a just pound, be it but so much
  As makes it light or heavy in the substance,
  Or the division of the twentieth part
  Of one poor scruple, nay if the scale do turn
  But in the estimation of a hair,
  Thou diest and all thy goods are confiscate.

Gratiano. A second Daniel, a Daniel, Jew!
  Now, infidel, I have you on the hip.

Portia. Why doth the Jew pause? Take thy forfeiture.

Shylock. Give me my principal, and let me go.

Bassanio. I have it ready for thee, here it is.

Portia. He hath refused it in the open court:
  He shall have merely justice and his bond.

Gratiano. Daniel, still say I, a second Daniel!
  I thank thee Jew for teaching me that word.

Shylock. Shall I not have barely my principal?

Portia. Thou shalt have nothing but the forfeiture
    To be so taken at thy peril, Jew.

Shylock. Why, then the devil give him good of it!
    I'll stay no longer question.

Portia.   Tarry, Jew,
    The law hath yet another hold on you.
    It is enacted in the laws of Venice,
    If it be proved against an alien
    That by direct or indirect attempts
    He seek the life of any citizen,
    The party 'gainst the which he doth contrive
    Shall seize one half his goods, the other half
    Comes to the privy coffer of the state,
    And the offender's life lies in the mercy
    Of the Duke only, 'gainst all other voice.
    In which predicament, I say, thou stand'st,
    For it appears by manifest proceeding,
    That indirectly, and directly too,
    Thou hast contrived against the very life
    Of the defendant, and thou hast incurr'd
    The danger formerly by me rehearsed.
    Down therefore, and beg mercy of the Duke.

Gratiano. Beg that thou mayst have leave to hang thyself:
    And yet thy wealth being forfeit to the state,
    Thou hast not left the value of a cord,
    Therefore thou must be hang'd at the state's charge.

Duke. That thou shalt see the difference of our spirit,
    I pardon thee thy life before thou ask it:
    For half thy wealth, it is Antonio's;
    The other half comes to the general state,
    Which humbleness may drive unto a fine.

Portia. Ay, for the state, not for Antonio.

Shylock. Nay, take my life and all, pardon not that:
    You take my house, when you do take the prop
    That doth sustain my house; you take my life
    When you do take the means whereby I live.

Portia. What mercy can you render him, Antonio?

Gratiano. A halter gratis, nothing else for God's sake.

Antonio. So please my lord the Duke and all the court
    To quit the fine for one half of his goods,
    I am content; so he will let me have
    The other half in use, to render it
    Upon his death, unto the gentleman
    That lately stole his daughter.
    Two things provided more, that for this favour
    He presently become a Christian;
    The other, that he do record a gift,
    Here in the court, of all he dies possess'd
    Unto his son Lorenzo and his daughter.

Duke. He shall do this, or else I do recant
    The pardon that I late pronounced here.

Portia. Art thou contented, Jew? What dost thou say?

Shylock. I am content.

Portia.   Clerk, draw a deed of gift.

Shylock. I pray you, give me leave to go from hence.
    I am not well: send the deed after me,
    And I will sign it.

Duke.   Get thee gone, but do it.

Gratiano. In christening shalt thou have two godfathers:
    Had I been judge, thou shouldst have had ten more,
    To bring thee to the gallows, not the font.

                          Exit Shylock.

Duke. Sir, I entreat you home with me to dinner.

Portia. I humbly do desire your Grace of pardon,
    I must away this night toward Padua,
    And it is meet I presently set forth.

Duke. I am sorry that your leisure serves you not.
    Antonio, gratify this gentleman,
    For, in my mind, you are much bound to him.

                          Exeunt Duke *and his train.*

Bassanio. Most worthy gentleman, I and my friend
    Have by your wisdom been this day acquitted
    Of grievous penalties, in lieu whereof,
    Three thousand ducats due unto the Jew
    We freely cope your courteous pains withal.

Antonio. And stand indebted, over and above,
    In love and service to you evermore.

Portia. He is well paid that is well satisfied,
    And I, delivering you, am satisfied
    And therein do account myself well paid:
    My mind was never yet more mercenary.
    I pray you, know me when we meet again.
    I wish you well, and so I take my leave.

Bassanio. Dear sir, of force I must attempt you further:
    Take some remembrance of us as a tribute,
    Not as a fee: grant me two things, I pray you,
    Not to deny me, and to pardon me.

Portia. You press me far, and therefore I will yield.
    [*To* Antonio] Give me your gloves, I'll wear them for your sake,
    [*To* Bassanio] And, for your love, I'll take this ring from you:
    Do not draw back your hand, I'll take no more,
    And you in love shall not deny me this.

Bassanio. This ring, good sir? Alas, it is a trifle!
   I will not shame myself to give you this.

Portia. I will have nothing else but only this,
   And now methinks I have a mind to it.

Bassanio. There's more depends on this than on the value.
   The dearest ring in Venice will I give you,
   And find it out by proclamation:
   Only for this, I pray you pardon me.

Portia. I see sir you are liberal in offers:
   You taught me first to beg, and now methinks
   You teach me how a beggar should be answer'd.

Bassanio. Good sir, this ring was given me by my wife,
   And when she put it on, she made me vow
   That I should neither sell nor give nor lose it.

Portia. That 'scuse serves many men to save their gifts.
   And if your wife be not a mad-woman,
   And know how well I have deserved the ring,
   She would not hold out enemy forever
   For giving it to me. Well, peace be with you!
                        Exeunt Portia *and* Nerissa.

Antonio. My Lord Bassanio, let him have the ring,
   Let his deservings and my love withal
   Be valued 'gainst your wife's commandment.

Bassanio. Go Gratiano, run and overtake him,
   Give him the ring, and bring him if thou canst
   Unto Antonio's house: away! Make haste.
                           Exit Gratiano.

   Come, you and I will thither presently,
   And in the morning early will we both
   Fly toward Belmont: come, Antonio.
                              Exeunt.

scene 2.   [*The same; A street*]

Enter Portia *and* Nerissa

Portia. Inquire the Jew's house out, give him this deed,
  And let him sign it: we'll away tonight
  And be a day before our husbands home:
  This deed will be well welcome to Lorenzo.
                              Enter Gratiano

Gratiano. Fair sir, you are well o'erta'en:
  My Lord Bassanio upon more advice
  Hath sent you here this ring, and doth entreat
  Your company at dinner.

Portia.   That cannot be:
  His ring I do accept most thankfully,
  And so I pray you tell him: furthermore,
  I pray you show my youth old Shylock's house.

Gratiano. That will I do.

Nerissa.   Sir, I would speak with you.
  [*Aside to* Portia] I'll see if I can get my husband's ring,
  Which I did make him swear to keep forever.

Portia. [*Aside to* Nerissa] Thou mayst, I warrant. We shall have
  old swearing
  That they did give the rings away to men,
  But we'll outface them, and outswear them too.
  [*Aloud*] Away! Make haste: thou know'st where I will tarry.

Nerissa. Come good sir, will you show me to this house?
                              Exeunt.

act 5

Enter Lorenzo *and* Jessica

Lorenzo. The moon shines bright. In such a night as this,
  When the sweet wind did gently kiss the trees
  And they did make no noise, in such a night
  Troilus methinks mounted the Trojan walls,
  And sigh'd his soul toward the Grecian tents
  Where Cressid lay that night.

Jessica.   In such a night
  Did Thisbe fearfully o'ertrip the dew,
  And saw the lion's shadow ere himself,
  And ran dismay'd away.

Lorenzo.   In such a night
  Stood Dido with a willow in her hand
  Upon the wild sea banks, and waft her love
  To come again to Carthage.

Jessica.   In such a night
  Medea gather'd the enchanted herbs
  That did renew old Æson.

Lorenzo.   In such a night
   Did Jessica steal from the wealthy Jew,
   And with an unthrift love did run from Venice
   As far as Belmont.

Jessica.   In such a night
   Did young Lorenzo swear he loved her well,
   Stealing her soul with many vows of faith
   And ne'er a true one.

Lorenzo.   In such a night
   Did pretty Jessica, like a little shrew,
   Slander her love, and he forgave it her.

Jessica. I would out-night you, did no body come,
   But hark, I hear the footing of a man.

                    Enter Stephano, *a messenger*

Lorenzo. Who comes so fast in silence of the night?

Stephano. A friend.

Lorenzo. A friend! What friend? Your name, I pray you friend?

Stephano. Stephano is my name, and I bring word
   My mistress will before the break of day
   Be here at Belmont: she doth stray about
   By holy crosses where she kneels and prays
   For happy wedlock hours.

Lorenzo.   Who comes with her?

Stephano. None but a holy hermit and her maid.
   I pray you, is my master yet return'd?

Lorenzo. He is not, nor we have not heard from him.
   But go we in, I pray thee Jessica,
   And ceremoniously let us prepare
   Some welcome for the mistress of the house.

                    Enter Launcelot

Launcelot. Sola, sola! Wo ha, ho! Sola, sola!

Lorenzo. Who calls?

Launcelot. Sola! Did you see Master Lorenzo? Master Lorenzo,
sola, sola!

Lorenzo. Leave hollaing, man: here.

Launcelot. Sola! Where? Where?

Lorenzo. Here!

Launcelot. Tell him there's a post come from my master, with his
horn full of good news: my master will be here ere morning.

Exit.

Lorenzo. Sweet soul, let's in, and there expect their coming.
And yet no matter: why should we go in?
My friend Stephano, signify, I pray you,
Within the house, your mistress is at hand,
And bring your music forth into the air.

Exit Stephano.

How sweet the moonlight sleeps upon this bank!
Here will we sit, and let the sounds of music
Creep in our ears: soft stillness and the night
Become the touches of sweet harmony.
Sit, Jessica. Look how the floor of heaven
Is thick inlaid with patens of bright gold:
There's not the smallest orb which thou behold'st
But in his motion like an angel sings,
Still quiring to the young-eyed cherubins;
Such harmony is in immortal souls,
But whilst this muddy vesture of decay
Doth grossly close it in, we cannot hear it.

Enter Musicians

Come, ho, and wake Diana with a hymn!
With sweetest touches pierce your mistress' ear,
And draw her home with music.

Music.

Jessica. I am never merry when I hear sweet music.

Lorenzo. The reason is, your spirits are attentive:
    For do but note a wild and wanton herd
    Or race of youthful and unhandled colts
    Fetching mad bounds, bellowing and neighing loud,
    Which is the hot condition of their blood;
    If they but hear perchance a trumpet sound,
    Or any air of music touch their ears,
    You shall perceive them make a mutual stand,
    Their savage eyes turn'd to a modest gaze
    By the sweet power of music: therefore the poet
    Did feign that Orpheus drew trees, stones, and floods,
    Since nought so stockish, hard, and full of rage,
    But music for the time doth change his nature.
    The man that hath no music in himself,
    Nor is not moved with concord of sweet sounds,
    Is fit for treasons, stratagems, and spoils;
    The motions of his spirit are dull as night,
    And his affections dark as Erebus:
    Let no such man be trusted. Mark the music.
               Enter Portia *and* Nerissa

Portia. That light we see is burning in my hall.
    How far that little candle throws his beams!
    So shines a good deed in a naughty world.

Nerissa. When the moon shone, we did not see the candle.

Portia. So doth the greater glory dim the less:
    A substitute shines brightly as a king,
    Until a king be by, and then his state
    Empties itself, as doth an inland brook
    Into the main of waters. Music! Hark!

Nerissa. It is your music, madam, of the house.

Portia. Nothing is good, I see, without respect:
   Methinks it sounds much sweeter than by day.

Nerissa. Silence bestows that virtue on it, madam.

Portia. The crow doth sing as sweetly as the lark
   When neither is attended, and I think
   The nightingale, if she should sing by day
   When every goose is cackling, would be thought
   No better a musician than the wren.
   How many things by season season'd are
   To their right praise and true perfection!
   Peace, ho! The moon sleeps with Endymion,
   And would not be awaked.

                                                Music ceases.

Lorenzo.   That is the voice,
   Or I am much deceived, of Portia.

Portia. He knows me as the blind man knows the cuckoo,
   By the bad voice.

Lorenzo.   Dear lady, welcome home!

Portia. We have been praying for our husbands' health,
   Which speed, we hope, the better for our words.
   Are they return'd?

Lorenzo.   Madam, they are not yet,
   But there is come a messenger before,
   To signify their coming.

Portia.   Go in, Nerissa.
   Give order to my servants that they take
   No note at all of our being absent hence;
   Nor you, Lorenzo; Jessica, nor you.

                                       A tucket sounds.

Lorenzo. Your husband is at hand, I hear his trumpet:
   We are no tell-tales, madam, fear you not.

Portia. This night methinks is but the daylight sick,
    It looks a little paler: 'tis a day,
    Such as the day is when the sun is hid.
        Enter Bassanio, Antonio, Gratiano, *and their followers*

Bassanio. We should hold day with the Antipodes,
    If you would walk in absence of the sun.

Portia. Let me give light, but let me not be light,
    For a light wife doth make a heavy husband,
    And never be Bassanio so for me.
    But God sort all! You are welcome home, my lord.

Bassanio. I thank you, madam. Give welcome to my friend.
    This is the man, this is Antonio,
    To whom I am so infinitely bound.

Portia. You should in all sense be much bound to him,
    For, as I hear, he was much bound for you.

Antonio. No more than I am well acquitted of.

Portia. Sir, you are very welcome to our house:
    It must appear in other ways than words,
    Therefore I scant this breathing courtesy.

Gratiano. [*To* Nerissa] By yonder moon I swear you do me
    wrong;
    In faith, I gave it to the judge's clerk:
    Would he were gelt that had it, for my part,
    Since you do take it, love, so much at heart.

Portia. A quarrel ho, already! What's the matter?

Gratiano. About a hoop of gold, a paltry ring
    That she did give me, whose posy was
    For all the world like cutler's poetry
    Upon a knife, 'Love me, and leave me not.'

Nerissa. What talk you of the posy or the value?
    You swore to me when I did give it you,

That you would wear it till your hour of death,
And that it should lie with you in your grave:
Though not for me, yet for your vehement oaths,
You should have been respective and have kept it.
Gave it a judge's clerk! No, God's my judge,
The clerk will ne'er wear hair on's face that had it.

Gratiano. He will, an if he live to be a man.

Nerissa. Ay, if a woman live to be a man.

Gratiano. Now, by this hand, I gave it to a youth,
A kind of boy, a little scrubbed boy
No higher than thyself, the judge's clerk,
A prating boy that begg'd it as a fee:
I could not for my heart deny it him.

Portia. You were to blame, I must be plain with you,
To part so slightly with your wife's first gift,
A thing stuck on with oaths upon your finger
And so riveted with faith unto your flesh.
I gave my love a ring, and made him swear
Never to part with it, and here he stands;
I dare be sworn for him he would not leave it
Nor pluck it from his finger, for the wealth
That the world masters. Now, in faith, Gratiano,
You give your wife too unkind a cause of grief,
An 'twere to me I should be mad at it.

Bassanio. [*Aside*] Why I were best to cut my left hand off,
And swear I lost the ring defending it.

Gratiano. My Lord Bassanio gave his ring away
Unto the judge that begg'd it, and indeed
Deserved it too; and then the boy, his clerk,
That took some pains in writing, he begg'd mine,
And neither man nor master would take aught
But the two rings.

Portia.   What ring gave you, my lord?
   Not that, I hope, which you received of me.

Bassanio. If I could add a lie unto a fault,
   I would deny it, but you see my finger
   Hath not the ring upon it, it is gone.

Portia. Even so void is your false heart of truth.
   By heaven I will ne'er come in your bed
   Until I see the ring.

Nerissa.   Nor I in yours
   Till I again see mine.

Bassanio.   Sweet Portia,
   If you did know to whom I gave the ring,
   If you did know for whom I gave the ring,
   And would conceive for what I gave the ring,
   And how unwillingly I left the ring,
   When nought would be accepted but the ring,
   You would abate the strength of your displeasure.

Portia. If you had known the virtue of the ring,
   Or half her worthiness that gave the ring,
   Or your own honour to contain the ring,
   You would not then have parted with the ring.
   What man is there so much unreasonable,
   If you had pleased to have defended it
   With any terms of zeal, wanted the modesty
   To urge the thing held as a ceremony?
   Nerissa teaches me what to believe:
   I'll die for't but some woman had the ring.

Bassanio. No by my honour madam, by my soul
   No woman had it, but a civil doctor,
   Which did refuse three thousand ducats of me,
   And begg'd the ring, the which I did deny him,

And suffer'd him to go displeased away,
Even he that did uphold the very life
Of my dear friend. What should I say, sweet lady?
I was enforced to send it after him,
I was beset with shame and courtesy;
My honour would not let ingratitude
So much besmear it. Pardon me good lady,
For by these blessed candles of the night,
Had you been there, I think you would have begg'd
The ring of me to give the worthy doctor.

Portia. Let not that doctor e'er come near my house.
Since he hath got the jewel that I loved,
And that which you did swear to keep for me,
I will become as liberal as you;
I'll not deny him anything I have,
No, not my body nor my husband's bed:
Know him I shall, I am well sure of it.
Lie not a night from home. Watch me like Argus:
If you do not, if I be left alone,
Now by mine honour, which is yet mine own,
I'll have that doctor for my bedfellow.

Nerissa. And I his clerk; therefore be well advised
How you do leave me to mine own protection.

Gratiano. Well, do you so: let not me take him then,
For if I do, I'll mar the young clerk's pen.

Antonio. I am th' unhappy subject of these quarrels.

Portia. Sir, grieve not you; you are welcome notwithstanding.

Bassanio. Portia, forgive me this enforced wrong,
And in the hearing of these many friends,
I swear to thee, even by thine own fair eyes
Wherein I see myself—

Portia.   Mark you but that!
   In both my eyes he doubly sees himself,
   In each eye, one: swear by your double self,
   And there's an oath of credit.

Bassanio.   Nay, but hear me:
   Pardon this fault, and by my soul I swear
   I never more will break an oath with thee.

Antonio. I once did lend my body for his wealth,
   Which but for him that had your husband's ring,
   Had quite miscarried. I dare be bound again,
   My soul upon the forfeit, that your lord
   Will never more break faith advisedly.

Portia. Then you shall be his surety. Give him this,
   And bid him keep it better than the other.

Antonio. Here Lord Bassanio, swear to keep this ring.

Bassanio. By heaven, it is the same I gave the doctor!

Portia. I had it of him: pardon me Bassanio,
   For by this ring the doctor lay with me.

Nerissa. And pardon me, my gentle Gratiano,
   For that same scrubbed boy, the doctor's clerk,
   In lieu of this, last night did lie with me.

Gratiano. Why, this is like the mending of highways
   In summer where the ways are fair enough!
   What, are we cuckolds ere we have deserved it?

Portia. Speak not so grossly. You are all amazed:
   Here is a letter; read it at your leisure.
   It comes from Padua, from Bellario:
   There you shall find that Portia was the doctor,
   Nerissa there her clerk. Lorenzo here
   Shall witness I set forth as soon as you,
   And even but now return'd; I have not yet